THEO-LOGY

How a Boy Wonder Led the Red Sox to the Promised Land

By John Frascella

CAMBRIDGE HOUSE PRESS

Published by
Cambridge House Press
www.camhousepress.com

Project Editor/Book Design: Rachel Trusheim.
Cover Design: Obtuse Lautrec.
Cover Image courtesy of Getty Images.
Photos on p 177, 201, 208: 2009 © Matt West.
Photos on p 68, 100, 193: 2009 © Rob Cuni.

Library of Congress Cataloging-in-Publication Data

Frascella, John.
  Theo-logy : how a boy wonder led the Red Sox to the promised land / by John Frascella.
      p. cm.
   ISBN 978-0-9814536-9-9 (pbk.)
   1. Epstein, Theo, 1973- 2. Boston Red Sox (Baseball team)--Management.
I. Title.

  GV865.E77F73 2009
  796.357092--dc22
  [B]

                                                          2009006840

978-0-9814536-9-9

Paperback original.

10 9 8 7 6 5 4 3 2 1

                    Printed in the United States of America.

For my always hip, never boring, one-in-a-trillion family:
Dad (John), Mom (Pauline), and sister (Melissa).
And you too, Red Sox Nation.

Acknowledgments

I'd like to credit my parents, Pauline and John, for raising me on baseball. Thanks to my uncles, Larry and Alan, for ushering me in this direction, and love to the rest of my family for always being there. Thanks to Summers, Fish, and Meyer for reading, and to Katie, Sam, Jimmy, and Frank for your friendship and love. Finally, a special thanks to Drew Nederpelt and Rachel Trusheim for your confidence in me, and your professionalism.

TABLE OF CONTENTS

Desperate Times Call for
Desperate Measures

On Halloween night of 2005, a gorilla got loose at Fenway. No, there wasn't a jailbreak at Boston's Franklin Park Zoo—this gorilla was in costume. As John Henry and many of the Red Sox's front office members mourned Theo Epstein's resignation, the media swarmed outside the stadium. The reporters waited for the Red Sox's suits to emerge from their haven, while the gorilla ran wild in the parking lot. Curiously steering clear of the media members, the giant ape lumbered toward some of the parked cars. Witnesses say the massive monkey got into a Volvo, and drove away quickly.

So who was the mysterious man in the gorilla suit?

He was the former general manager of the Boston Red Sox. In a successful effort to avoid the media onslaught, Theo borrowed the costume from a (former) colleague at Fenway, suited up, and scurried to the safety of his car.

Less than three years later, Theo was back in baseball.

As the general manager of the Boston Red Sox, he is regarded by many as one of the best—if not, *the* best—GMs in the big leagues. With a wonderful family, an enviable job, and a pair of gorgeous World Series rings, life is good for Theo Epstein. It's not uncommon for a Bostonian to say, "What I wouldn't do to switch places with him…"

But why did Theo leave in 2005, and what brought him back early in '06?

That question and many more will be answered as you progress through this book. Theo has been described by a close family friend as "brilliant, but a little bit crazy." The brilliance and craziness that has encapsulated the life of Theo Epstein, and the play of his Boston Red Sox, are spotlighted in the coming chapters.

"The Wonder Kid," Literally

Please brace yourselves for this one, Red Sox fans: Theo Nathan Epstein, Boston's golden boy, architect of the 2004 and 2007 World Series championship teams, was born December 29, 1973...

In New York City.

That's right, Red Sox Nation, your beloved general manager is a native New Yorker—a natural-born Yankee.

Gulp.

If you're forced to look at Theo differently now, well, the facts are what they are. You're just gonna have to try to live it down. It'll be difficult to shake at first, but rest assured, the World Series victories will help you forget.

Theo was born to proud parents, Leslie and Ilene Epstein, but wasn't the only reason for his parents to be prideful on December 29, 1973. Theo emerged 10 seconds after his older twin brother, Paul.

"Paul" was a simple enough choice, but why the name "Theo"? The Epsteins have an interesting reason:

"Theo was conceived in Holland, and we wanted to give our child a Dutch name," said Leslie in an interview with the *Yale Daily News*. "Theo was popular at the time, and it also happened to be the name of Van Gogh's brother."

Even before he was born, Theo was linked to a prodigy. That shouldn't surprise anyone; he always seems to be a little ahead of the game.

The Epstein family tree is quite a fascinating one. Theo was born into an intriguing family of intellectual, literary minds. His grandfather, Philip Epstein, co-wrote the screenplay for the classic Warner Bros. film, *Casablanca*. Philip's partner in crime was *his* twin, Theo's great-uncle, Julius. *Casablanca* starred Humphrey Bogart and Ingrid Bergman and won the 1943 Academy Award for Outstanding Motion Picture.

But Outstanding Motion Picture wasn't the only victory for *Casablanca* at the Oscars—Phillip and Julius took home the Academy Award for Best Screenplay.

"The Academy Award, which actually rests in the den at my parent's place, represents our grandfather and our great uncle. So nothing would ever trump that," Theo told the Associated Press in his first year as general manager. "But I think we can make room for a World Series trophy."

Make it two, Theo.

Today, *Casablanca* is considered an absolute must-see film, and one of the best stories ever written for the big screen. In fact, it made the top five on the American Film Institute's "100 Greatest Movies of All Time" list.

Having a famous grandfather had its advantages.

"[*Casablanca*] was just sort of a neat part of family history that I could use to meet girls," Theo said. His grandfather went on to write for films like *Mr. Skeffington* (1944) and *My Foolish Heart* (1949), but none of his subsequent works could match the success or acclaim of *Casablanca*. This is not a slight on Philip or Julius; *Casablanca* is a true masterpiece, and it was likely impossible to conjure a work of equal value or impact.

Philip's son and Theo's father, Leslie, has been the director of the Creative Writing program at Boston University for over 20 years. After growing up in California, he switched coasts to pursue an undergraduate degree at Yale. (As you read on you'll find that, in more ways than one, Yale has had a profound impact on Theo's life.) Leslie thrived at Yale, and used his undergraduate degree as a gateway to Oxford University, arguably the most prestigious academic institution in the world. As a Rhodes Scholar, Leslie is in the impressive company of influential astronomer Edwin Hubble, former U.S. senator J. William Fulbright (the name upon the now-famous Fulbright scholarships) and former U.S. president Bill Clinton.

Leslie has published nine fiction books, the most notable of which is *The King of the Jews*, a Holocaust novel that was highly controversial at the time of its release in 1979, but one that has since been printed in over 10 different languages. Despite the controversy in its opening year, *The King of the Jews* was a *New York Times* bestseller and is now considered one of the essential literary works about the harsh realities and undeniable horrors of the Holocaust.

Theo's older sister, Anya, also inherited the literary genes. She wrote scripts for the dramatic television series, *Homicide: Life on the Street*. The show ran from 1993 to 1999, and won four Primetime Emmys along the way.

Anya's husband, Dan Futterman, is another highly successful writer. He was an actor on TV shows like *Judging Amy* and *Will & Grace*, but his ultimate claim to fame is the screenplay to the 2005 film, *Capote*. Like Anya's grandfather and great-uncle, her husband was nominated for Best Screenplay at the Academy Awards. Unfortunately, Futterman was unable to follow in the footsteps of Philip and Julius Epstein by winning the Oscar; the award went to the writers of *Brokeback Mountain*.

Anya and Dan have two daughters, Eve and Sylvie. In addition to the girls, Theo has another niece and nephew. His brother, Paul, and sister-in-law, Saskia, have a daughter, Annika, and son, Ezra.

Theo's mother, Ilene, isn't a successful screenwriter, author, poet, or anything of the sort, but she's certainly a successful businesswoman. Ilene runs The Studio, a popular women's clothing store in Brookline, Massachusetts, that "has it all: clothes for work, play, and evenings out," according to the official website. Fittingly enough, Ilene controls the store along with her twin sister, Sandy. (Yes, a third pair of twins on the extended Epstein family tree.) Ilene and Sandy work with a partner, close family friend Marcie Brawer.

Theo's life began on the Upper West Side of Manhattan, where Leslie and Ilene got to know one another. Sandy had been taking a few classes at the nearby Queens College, one of which was a course in adult education. Her instructor was an intriguing man, a man who seemed almost too clever, intelligent, and witty to be teaching at QC. Queens College was no joke, but as far as academics went, it wasn't exactly Yale University. Seeming both knowledgeable and worldly, this particular teacher stuck out like a sore thumb.

The man behind the podium, of course, was Leslie. Sandy eventually introduced him to her sister, and Leslie and Ilene hit it off immediately. The two have been together ever since.

Leslie and Ilene decided to move their lives and family to Boston in 1978. Theo had spent four years in New York, but don't worry, Sox fans, he wasn't infected by the poisonous navy blue pinstripes. Leslie absolutely despises the Yankees, and would never have allowed Theo to walk to the doorstep of the Evil Empire. He introduced Theo and Paul to baseball, and taught them how to enjoy the beauty of each and every play. Having grown up a fan of the Hollywood Stars, a minor league team in the Pacific Coast League, Leslie, too, developed his affinity for the game at a young age. He moved on from the Stars when he came to the East Coast, where the Red Sox eventually captured his heart.

Unfortunately for Leslie, he and his family were greeted rudely in Boston—1978 was the year of the infamous Bucky Dent home run. In a one-game playoff determining the fates of the Red Sox and Yankees, New York defeated Boston on the strength of Dent's three-run shot in the seventh inning off hurler Mike Torrez. The Yankees had been trailing 2-0, and Dent was hitting just .243 on the season. The scrappy little infielder sent the Sox, and their fans, home crying. He was a hero so unlikely that then-Red Sox skipper Don Zimmer (who eventually became the Yankees' bench coach) could only shake his head and say, "Bucky Fucking Dent."

Dent had Leslie shaking his head as well, but at least the Epsteins were out of New York. Besides, it couldn't get much worse for the Red Sox next year, could it?

Well, it would be awhile before the Sox turned things around. In the meantime, Theo and his siblings grew up comfortably in their Brookline apartment on Parkman Street.

Theo has fond memories of those times.

"When I think of my family, I think of my dad cooped in his office, writing about a sentence a day; my mom rushing home from work to make an unbelievable dinner in 30 minutes; my sister locked in her room listening to really bad pop music; and my brother and I beating the heck out of each other in the hallway," he said.

OK, maybe "fond" isn't the best word, but funny at least.

Living about a block away from Fenway Park it was no wonder that, over the years, Theo's interest in baseball blossomed into an intense passion, bordering on obsession.

"If my mom wanted to go vacuum or do some housework and leave me occupied, she would turn on the baseball game and that would be it for a couple of hours," Theo said. "My dad tells stories of me early on aligning the defense in the outfield [during a televised game]."

Theo and Paul attended over a dozen Red Sox home games per season, often escorted by their father. By the time they were teenagers, both brothers would be completely immersed in the action. Paul was a little behind; Theo was locked into every pitch before reaching the age of 10.

Theo recalled those days.

"By the third inning, Paul would be reading *Highlights* magazine," Theo said. "I would be keeping score for the whole nine innings."

Most nine-year-olds can't focus long enough to keep score for an inning, let alone an entire game. Theo's intense scorekeeping was a small but interesting indication of things to come.

It was around that point in his life that Theo realized his dream: he wanted to be involved in the world of sports. Ilene has told people that Theo said he "wouldn't be happy unless he worked in sports," as early as age eight or nine. Theo longed to be the Red Sox's starting shortstop, but knew it would be a difficult dream to achieve. If he couldn't make it on the field, Theo just wanted a job in sports, somewhere. It's almost as if he realized that the goal of playing in the pros was too lofty. But then again, he would eventually aspire to become the general manager of the Boston Red Sox—not exactly the most realistic goal, either.

A few years later, as he closed in on the ever-confusing teenage era, Theo suffered the first significant injury of his sports career. No, he wasn't hit with a line drive or a wild pitch; in fact, he wasn't even on the baseball field. While playing soccer, Theo had the skin sliced above his eye. As a result, he was forced to pick up a pair of sports goggles. Doing his best Kurt Rambis or Horace Grant impersonation, Theo played in the goofy goggles for much of his athletic life. It wasn't the most attractive look, but what did the ladies think?

"Did girls like him? Kinda, sorta," said former classmate Tessa Skinner in *Boston Magazine*. "Some girls thought he was cute. He was this skinny kid with glasses. When he ditched the glasses later in high school, he got a little more popular."

When young Theo wasn't at Fenway for a Sox game, he was watching them on TV in the Epsteins' den. He would be glued to the screen—often with Paul by his side—until trouble arose. Not trouble in the form of a Red Sox blunder, but trouble in the form of Anya.

Hey, she needed some TV time too.

Anya was the eldest of the three, but she was often overruled by the twins. The night of a Red Sox game, which was virtually every night of the summer, Anya was lucky to get an hour with the television. Theo just wasn't having it. Paul would be right there backing him up.

But Theo's precious TV time did not come without a price. For every minute of television, Leslie made Theo read a page in a book. Sometimes in the middle of a game, after the first few innings, Leslie would ask Theo to make up for the time—a serious bummer for one of Red Sox Nation's most enthusiastic members.

Well, not exactly. Rather easily, Theo would sidle around his father's orders.

"It wasn't that hard to beat the system," Theo said. "I would lock myself up in my room with a book, rustling the pages loudly while quietly listening to the game on the radio."

But Theo wasn't always ignoring the book in hand. He and his siblings were very accomplished young readers.

"We read most of the classics by the time we were through with elementary school," he added.

When it came to following the Red Sox, if Theo wasn't at Fenway, he was watching on television. If it wasn't the TV, it was the radio. No matter what the circumstances, he did everything in his power to catch every inning of every game. Eight years after the Epsteins arrived in Boston, and five years after he began to live and die with every pitch, Theo was rewarded for his dedication to the Red Sox. Unfortunately, severe punishment followed the reward.

In 1986, Theo's boys went 95-66 in the regular season, finishing first in the American League Eastern Division, ahead of the bone-headed Bombers from the Bronx. In a dramatic seven-game series, the Sox defeated the California Angels in the American League Championship Series. Theo was at Fenway for game 7 of the ALCS for what, up to that point, was unquestionably the most significant Red Sox game of his life. After the convincing 8-1 victory he watched his favorite players celebrate and mob each other, and with that, Theo had reached his first World Series. It was as a fan, but nonetheless he was World Series bound.

The Red Sox opened the series in New York, beginning their epic battle with the Big Apple's other team, the Mets. The Sox took both games at Shea Stadium, stunning the Met faithful and stealing away the home field advantage. It had been 68 years since the Red Sox's last World Series title, but '86 was beginning to look like a year for fine wine. The Sox and Mets were on their way to Fenway for game 3… and so was Theo.

Theo and his family were in attendance for the first World Series game at Fenway Park since 1975, and if the Red Sox could pull off the victory, they could stick a fork in the Metropolitans. In the history of Major League Baseball, no team had ever come back from a 3-0 hole to win a postseason series. Only two teams in the four major sports—baseball, basketball, football, hockey—had ever erased such a deficit: the 1942 Toronto Maple Leafs and the 1975 New York Islanders. (Of course, the 2004 Red Sox would add themselves to this list, but they couldn't help Theo back in '86.)

In his seat at Fenway, young Theo bit his nails throughout game 3—he shouldn't have bothered. With their backs against the wall, the Mets responded, spanking the Red Sox by the score of 7-1. The outcome was never in doubt. New York scored four first inning runs off Boston starter Dennis "Oil Can" Boyd, and the early offensive outburst would prove to be more than enough for the Mets to secure the victory. The Sox failed to employ the foot-on-the-throat mentality, and Theo's first World Series game at Fenway ended in complete and utter disappointment.

On the bright side, the Sox held a 2-1 series lead and they'd have another shot to protect their home field in game 4. Sadly for Theo, they wouldn't protect much of anything. The Mets cleaned house again, winning 6-2 at Fenway. The home team lost the first four games of the '86 World Series, but the unusual streak finally snapped in game 5, when the Red Sox won 4-2 in Boston.

Theo was one win away from his first World Series championship as a part of Red Sox Nation.

October 25, 1986, the date of the now-infamous game 6. That night, Theo and Paul sweated over every pitch, and it looked as if they were going to be rewarded for their rigorous rooting effort. The Red Sox carried a 5-3 lead into the bottom of the tenth inning with their 6-foot-4 right-hander Calvin Schiraldi on the hill. Schiraldi was in the midst of his breakout season, a year in which he posted an anemic 1.41 ERA with 55 strikeouts in 51 innings of work, and he had already thrown two innings in game 6. He allowed a run to score on a sac fly in the bottom of the eighth, but followed up with a scoreless ninth inning.

Schiraldi had been Boston's most dominant relief pitcher, and he appeared to have settled down in the ninth; he was a shoe-in to hold a two-run lead.

Theo's hopes were up. And then, in the bottom of the tenth…Well, you know… Bill Buckner.

Theo and Paul saw it all happen in the den of the Epsteins' apartment. Their couch was the deathbed of the 1986 Red Sox's season. Their championship dreams were buried on the floor, next to the couch. Theo recalled the experience for *Boston Globe* columnist Dan Shaughnessy in his 2005 book, *Reversing the Curse*:

"We were on that couch for about 40 minutes, and when the ball rolled through Buckner's legs we just crumbled to the floor, holding our stomachs in disbelief. We sat for a few minutes and then the phone rang, and it was my dad's cousin Jimmy calling from California to taunt us."

Funny cousin. Sure, Boston had a chance to redeem itself in game 7 at Shea, but many Red Sox fans felt the series ended with Buckner.

And it did. The Mets proceeded to pound out eight

runs en route to a three-run victory in game 7 of the '86 World Series. For the first time, Theo experienced the suffering that exemplified life as a die-hard Red Sox fan from 1919 to 1985. It was a horrible feeling—a fan's rock bottom. Theo's first love had broken his heart into little, tiny pieces.

But she would be back. As for rock bottom, Theo would get to experience the exact opposite in the future. He'd have to work to get there, though.

In the meantime, *The Wonder Years* confronted "The Wonder Boy." While his classmates struggled with their identities, Theo continued on a path that was established during his childhood.

"He wasn't a big partier," said George Borokhov, an old pal. "He took a lot of AP classes. He didn't have girls around him."

When he wasn't reading, studying or watching the Red Sox, Theo was battling Paul in basketball. The twins had a little hoop set up in the hallway of the Epsteins' apartment, and they used it for some friendly one-on-one games—minus the "friendly." The boys would get loud and physical to the point where neighbors would have to intervene.

"You guys are 15 years old! You should be out drinking beer and chasing girls!" one neighbor complained.

Instead of indulging in the intrigue of underage drinking, Theo and his boys would spend their free time at Boston Billiards, or the Village Fare Pizza place. Eggs that soared and smashed into car doors on Halloween represented the pinnacle of mischief in Theo's life. What a rebel.

Simultaneously, the wheels on Theo's own baseball career were spinning. Eh, "spinning" is probably not the best word, more like "sputtering." To Theo's credit, things looked promising early on... *really* early on.

"Crowds used to gather and kind of watch, so I think maybe I did peak at about age four, baseball-wise," Theo told the Associated Press about his wiffleball days.

The other highlight of Theo's playing career was when his youth team won the city championship in the Brookline Pony League. Like most young ballplayers, Theo had the versatility to play adequately at a number of different positions. He was a two-way player, a pitcher and infielder. As a pitcher, he was one of the only kids in the league to throw a curveball. For once, Theo was a little *too* far ahead of the game—the breaking ball led to arm trouble (the second and most devastating injury of his athletic career), decreased velocity, and weakened all-around performance.

There are two interesting things to note about that team: (1) one of Theo's teammates was Sam Kennedy. Yup, that Sam Kennedy, now executive vice president and chief sales and marketing officer of the Boston Red Sox... talk about taking care of your friends. Theo was a solid player on the team, but Kennedy was a stud. The separation in ability between the two would hold steady throughout their playing careers.

And (2), their team name was the Yankees. C'mon, Red Sox fans, Theo was born in New York City and he played for the Yankees as a kid. His true loyalties may be in question.

After the Pony League, Theo's ballplayer life faded away—thus "sputtering," not "spinning." He managed to make a team every year at Brookline High School, but was never much of a factor on the field. Theo spent his first two seasons on the junior varsity squad, where he received a decent amount of playing time, and did little with it. He was a Punch-and-Judy hitter with a batting average hovering around .250. Major league scouts weren't exactly lining up to see Theo play.

Following a couple of average seasons in the JV league, Theo made the jump up to the varsity. The playing time he saw on JV… not quite there at the next level. Theo was one of the last guys on the bench, a backup middle in-fielder and a mop-up pitcher in blowout affairs. Kennedy still had it though; he was the starting shortstop.

Riding the pine may have put a few splinters in Theo's behind, but he wasn't complete deadwood for the Brookline High School varsity baseball team. He found a way to make himself useful: waiving runners home from the coach's box on the third-base side of the diamond. Teammates said Theo was a very effective third base coach; it seems that he was always fit for management. Like his scorekeeping at Fenway Park, this was another sign of things to come in Theo's life.

He may not have been a decorated baseball player, but Theo could certainly kick around a soccer ball. In 1991, his senior year, Theo was an integral part of the Brookline Warriors futbol club. The Warriors worked all the way up to the state tournament, and Theo was a key contributor to their success.

Naturally, as Theo's soccer and baseball careers came to a close, his high school academic career followed suit. He breezed through the four years, barely breaking a sweat. It was an impressive achievement, because Brookline was considered one of the better high schools in the entire state of Massachusetts. Theo made a challenging curriculum look like a walk in the park, and would soon follow in his father's Ivy League footsteps. He scored a near 1500 on the SATs, and in his high school yearbook, Theo claimed his favorite saying to be: "I got into Yale early!"

Other famous Brookline High grads include Conan O'Brien, funny man and host of NBC's *Late Night with Conan O'Brien*; Lew Schneider, writer and producer of the critically acclaimed sitcom, *Everybody Loves Raymond*; and Robert Kraft, owner of Gillette Stadium in Foxboro, the three-time Super Bowl champion New England Patriots, and Major League Soccer's New England Revolution.

Today, Theo's brother, Paul, works at Brookline High as a social worker and assistant soccer coach. Bumper stickers around the school parking lot read, "Our General Manager Was Student of the Month at Brookline High School."

After leaving his mark at Brookline High, Theo went

from Massachusetts down to Connecticut. The fall se-
mester of 1991 was the first for Theo at Yale, one of the
premier universities in the country. Theo would have to
perform to the school's high academic standards, but it
wouldn't be much of a problem for him.

Theo declared himself an American Studies major.
Yale's American Studies program is one of the oldest and
most storied in the country: introduced in the late 1940s,
it is interdisciplinary, and offers courses in art and American history, literature, film, sociology, political science,
and more. For a student with an open mind, the program's
possibilities are endless.

But Theo just wasn't that type of student. When it
came to devoting his effort and energy, his mind rested
comfortably on the "closed" side; more often than not, his
thoughts were of baseball.

Theo cruised as an American Studies major, but he
didn't exactly make a name for himself in the program. After asking around, Victorine Shepard, one of the current
administrators for Yale's American Studies department,
said there "was debate as to whether or not Mr. Epstein
graduated from our program." Some members of the department said they heard that Theo was a history major.

Hmm. Don't programs usually keep track of their
noteworthy or famous graduates? Her response seemed
odd. It seemed even more peculiar when Shepard admitted that she was a devoted Red Sox fan, as were the vast
majority of her colleagues in the department.

American Studies chairperson Matthew Jacobson initially said, "What years was Theo here?—I had no idea," and after talking to colleagues added that he was "shocked" that none of his faculty members knew of Theo's graduation from their program. He found it peculiar because some of his coworkers have been in the department for a long time, long enough to have been there when Theo was a student.

In her office at Yale, Shepard has a picture of herself, American Studies professor Michael Denning, and History professor John Demos with Larry Lucchino, president and CEO of the Boston Red Sox, holding the 2004 World Series trophy. After the victory in '04, Lucchino, who graduated from Yale Law School in 1971, decided to show the trophy off on his old stomping grounds, and bask in its glory with fellow Red Sox supporters. He found more than a few avid members of Red Sox Nation in the American Studies department.

"I have my summer mornings planned," Shepard said. "I have three routines. I have one kind of morning when the Red Sox win and the Yankees lose. I have another one when they both win and another one when the Yankees win and the Red Sox lose. [For the third one] I watch no sports shows that morning."

Yet she didn't know that Theo Epstein, the general manager of her beloved team, graduated from her program? Most of her colleagues weren't sure, either? This is no slight on Ms. Shepard or the other members of the

American Studies department—not at all, actually—the point here is, Theo certainly didn't leave much of an impression. Academically, he was just another face in the crowd. The professors who were in the department from '91 to '95 don't go around telling stories like, "When I first met Theo…" or "you should have seen Theo this one time…"

And that's because there are no stories.

After a double check of the records, Shepard was able to verify that Theo did, in fact, graduate from the American Studies program.

All right, so he didn't spend much time schmoozing administrators and other superiors. Not a big deal. Maybe Theo made his mark in the classroom, with the professors who actually taught him. Demos, who was in the photo with Lucchino and the World Series trophy, has been working at Yale for over 20 years.

"Somebody told me that [Theo] took my course," said Demos.

Someone told him that, but Demos doesn't remember teaching a student by the name of Theo Epstein. Today, he knows that name very well. Demos is a huge Red Sox fan who said he feels like he owes something to Theo in lieu of his favorite team's success.

"I've been a Red Sox fan since I was nine years old in 1946," Demos said. "And I fully expected that I would never see them win the championship after so many years; let alone twice. I feel in debt to Theo, I don't know how else to say it."

So Theo Epstein, the general manager, is held in extremely high regard at Yale. As for Theo Epstein, the student… well, that's a different story. It's almost as if he didn't exist.

"I've heard a good deal of hallway conversations the last several years like, 'Did you know Theo Epstein?' Demos said. But I can't recall anybody who has claimed to know him personally."

Jacobson has a theory about Theo's mysterious tenure in his department.

"We get two kind of students," Jacobson said, "We get really, really serious people who take on the spirit of the program, work very hard, and go on to do pretty amazing things in law, politics, teaching, and more. Then we get another kind of student—the kind that it seems [Theo] was—who wander into it because they like the fact that they can take anything, learn a little of this, a little of that, but tend to simply find a way to skate through."

Jacobson may very well have hit the nail on the head, but there was another reason why Theo was M.I.A.—he was making connections elsewhere. Theo wanted to get inside baseball, and knew the Yale American Studies department wasn't a direct pathway to his dreams. In 1992, he wrote a letter to the Baltimore Orioles, a team that played in the American League Eastern Division—the same division as the Yankees and Red Sox. There was nothing random about this letter, or the organization he decided to write it to; Theo had done his homework. He hoped to get his foot in the door by impressing with his writing and ambition, and appealing to some of the Yale graduates in Baltimore's front office. (More on this in the next chapter.)

Theo was also getting his name out there as a sports columnist and editor for the *Yale Daily News*. He was known to tackle the big issues, and wasn't exactly one for "fluff journalism"—that is, journalism that always pumped up or supported the Yale athletic teams, their players and coaches alike. Theo told it like it was. The column gave him an opportunity to have his voice heard, and he wasn't going to waste that opportunity by whispering or mumbling. In his stories, Theo spoke loudly and clearly.

One piece in particular, previewing the 1993 Harvard-Yale football game, created quite a stir. The title of the piece was, "Is It Time for Carm to Go?" "Carm" was Carmen Cozza, Yale's head football coach, winner of 10 Ivy League championships and a member of the College Football Hall of Fame. Cozza won 179 games in his illustrious career, finishing 60 games over the .500 mark. He was an icon at Yale, and Theo wanted him gone. Theo questioned Cozza's passion and ability to motivate his players, and blamed him for the team's struggles.

The day Theo's piece was published—gameday—he made a stop at the Yale press box prior to the action. He carried copies of his stories with him, and energetically passed them out to the members of the press in attendance. One of the copies was handed to Dan Shaughnessy, a renowned columnist. Little did Theo know that, in the future, he would sit down with Shaughnessy to discuss his life for the aforementioned book, *Reversing the Curse*. At the time, he introduced himself to Shaughnessy and moved on to his next victim.

Recently, Shaughnessy recalled his initial meeting with Theo.

"He was probably only about 19 at the time, but I could tell [Theo] was a smart young guy," said Shaughnessy. "He wrote a good piece. He would have been a hell of a writer."

Yale went on to squeak out a 33-31 victory over Harvard that day, and Cozza wasn't going anywhere. In fact, he'd outlast Theo at Yale—Theo graduated in 1995, and Cozza retired after the '96 season. Yale's athletic department could never fire him. Legend around the Yale campus is that after the game, Cozza said, "We ought to give that damn kid the ball."

Take that, Theo. So Theo's column didn't cause a violent and immediate overthrow, but it did earn him a parting shot from a Hall of Fame coach. It also got him noticed. No one from the American Studies department seems to remember him from back then, but Shaughnessy certainly does.

Theo enjoyed the microphone that a column provided him with but ultimately decided against a career in journalism. He found sportswriting to be an "individualistic pursuit," and foresaw a life of loneliness in such a field.

Theo wanted to interact with people; he wanted a life of excitement.

The Cozza article isn't the only thing people remember about Theo's days on the *Yale Daily News* staff. The editor-in-chief at the time, Emily Nelson, said Theo was never shy about his *true* aspirations. She said Theo used to tell everyone that, after his days at Yale, he was going to be the Boston Red Sox's general manager. There wasn't a single member of the staff who didn't respect Theo's intelligence or his ability as a writer, but they had no choice but to dismiss his Red Sox dreams. It was a goal too lofty, too improbable for anyone to take him seriously.

"I took Theo's Red Sox GM bit much in the same vein as other students' desires to be president or governor," Nelson said.

Other members of the *Daily News* staff remembered Theo for his humor.

"Theo was very, very funny," recalled Noah Bookbinder, who was the paper's managing editor. "He could be very irreverent, coming up with inside jokes, plays on words, physical joking—he was very charismatic."

In addition to the newspaper, Theo worked in the Sports Information department and was the student manager of the men's hockey team. Many of his good friends were hockey players, and Theo would occasionally attend the team's raucous parties. Even there, Theo remained reserved. Friends said he would come to hang out, but let them do all of the crazy, stereotypical college kid stuff.

Theo also spent a little time with the ladies. He had a few girlfriends along the way, but found himself getting bored with them rather quickly. Theo has said that his relationships rarely lasted past the half-year mark. Everything considered—the girls, friends, newspaper, and two other jobs—there wasn't much time for studying. His father remembers well:

"He wasn't into grades," Leslie said. "I told him, the one course he absolutely had to take was Scully's History of Art, and of course he didn't do that."

History of Art aside, Theo graduated from Yale in May of 1995. Soon after, his baseball career would receive a jolt, one that would propel him on the way to making history of his own.

From Baltimore, to San Diego, to Boston

Theo Epstein broke into baseball with one little piece of paper. That piece of paper, the letter he wrote to the Baltimore Orioles early in 1992, could have easily been lost in the shuffle of thousands upon thousands of letters the Orioles received every day. But using his university as leverage, Theo made sure that it didn't. There were a few Yale graduates in the Orioles' front office, and Theo had a plan to reach them. Before he knew it, he'd be working alongside of them.

The first Yalie was Calvin Hill—yes, that Calvin Hill—former NFL running back of the Dallas Cowboys, Washington Redskins, and Cleveland Browns. Hill rushed for over 6,000 yards in his career, and was selected for the Pro Bowl (the NFL equivalent of the MLB All-Star Game) four times. When his playing days were over, Hill made the professional jump from the NFL to Major League Baseball. At the time of Theo's letter, Hill was the Orioles' vice president of Administrative Personnel.

Then there was Dr. Charles Steinberg. Steinberg was the Orioles' director of Public Affairs, responsible for four departments in the organization. He began his career in baseball as an intern with the Orioles in 1976, when he was just 17 years of age. Steinberg started as the club's stat guy, and worked his way up from there. With some last-minute scouting help, he caught the eye of Hall of Fame manager Earl Weaver during the 1979 American League Championship Series. After that, there was nowhere to go but up. Steinberg is now the executive vice president and chief marketing officer for the Los Angeles Dodgers, and was the Red Sox's vice president of Public Affairs before that.

Last was Larry Lucchino—yup, the same guy from the photo in Victorine Shepard's office at Yale. Lucchino was president and part owner of the Orioles when Theo Epstein's name was first whispered. In 1979, he began working for the Orioles as vice president and general counsel. Unlike Steinberg, Lucchino didn't have to work his way up the ladder—he started near the very top. Now Lucchino is the president and CEO of the Red Sox.

Initially, Theo's fate was in the hands of Calvin Hill—literally. Hill was the one who walked Theo's letter into Steinberg's office. In exactly the manner he expected, Theo caught Hill's eye.

"One of the things that struck me was that he was a Yalie," Hill told the *Yale Daily News*.

Theo had played the Yale card to perfection. Like Hill,

Steinberg approved of Theo's Bulldog background, and of course, he too had started at the bottom as a young intern with the Orioles. Naturally Steinberg was reminded of his own past, and wanted to help Theo get the same opportunity for his future. He did so by scheduling a meeting with Theo for early in 1992.

While Theo was away at school, Steinberg interviewed hundreds and hundreds of internship candidates. After awhile it became easy for him to identify an average candidate, and unfortunately, he found that most candidates were exactly that. When Theo sat down with him for the first time during spring break of '92 (while his friends were in Cancun partying hard) Steinberg saw a young man who was anything but average. This kid was unique. Steinberg was intrigued by Theo's ability to articulate complex and unusual ideas.

Hill was also excited about the freshman from Yale. Theo was studied in the works of Bill James, an influential baseball author, historian, and theorist who questioned some of the game's universally accepted strategies and methods. He was particularly knowledgeable of *The Bill James Historical Baseball Abstract* from 1985. In that book James ranked the greatest players of all time, and included more than a few names from the Negro Leagues. James' descriptions of the players and stories from their league intrigued Theo, so much so that he spent free time looking deeper into the unfairly vague history of the Negro Leagues.

Hill, an African-American, said, "Theo was a base-ball historian and knew a lot about the Negro League[s], which also impressed me."

After his meeting with Theo was over, Hill told Stein-berg that he was reminded of an old friend, Mr. A. Bartlett Giamatti, a gentleman better known as "Bart."

"Whoever I can compare to Bart, I find favorable," Hill said.

Bart was the father of Paul Giamatti, the actor noted for his fine work in films like *Sideways* (2004) and *Cinder-ella Man* (2005). Paul also appeared on a television show called *Homicide: Life on the Street*—the very show that Theo's sister, Anya, wrote scripts for. Ah, the connections. As for Bart, he graduated from Yale in 1960, and eventu-ally became the seventh commissioner in the history of Major League Baseball. Oh yeah, he was the president of Yale before that, too.

Quite clearly, A. Bartlett Giamatti was a name that could never be thrown around lightly. This was a man loved by virtually all who came in contact with him, a man who appreciated the minutiae of baseball, one who was at home in the office of the commissioner. He would never hesitate to write about baseball:

> It breaks your heart. It is designed to break your heart. The game begins in the spring, when ev-erything else begins again, and it blossoms in the summer, filling the afternoons and evenings, and then as soon as the chill rains come, it stops and

leaves you to face the fall alone. You count on it, rely on it to buffer the passage of time, to keep the memory of sunshine and high skies alive, and then just when the days are all twilight, when you need it most, it stops. Today, October 2, a Sunday of rain and broken branches and leaf-clogged drains and slick streets, it stopped, and summer was gone.

If you love baseball, down to every last detail, then reading that hurts. It's that sinking feeling that sets in when the season ends, and all that's ahead is another autumn followed by seemingly endless winter. The above was an excerpt from Giamatti's piece, "The Green Fields of the Mind."

Bart Giamatti was a thoughtful, intelligent man, who, some believe, died of a broken heart. Just eight days after banishing Pete Rose from baseball, a heart attack took Giamatti's life at his vacation home in Martha's Vineyard. With 4,256 career hits, Rose was the all-time major league leader—but he bet on baseball. Reports were that Rose disgraced the game even further by betting on his own team, the Reds. (In 2007, Rose said he was wrong, and admitted to betting on his team "every night.") Giamatti had handled the situation correctly, but it pained him to dismiss a player who, in between the lines, always played the game as it was supposed to be played: hard, and as if every out was his last. "Charlie Hustle" was a legend, and to do what was right, Giamatti had to kick him to the curb. Giamatti said he suffered through the decision-making process in "silent agony."

On September 1, 1989, in Martha's Vineyard, baseball lost one of its great ambassadors too soon. Of interest, Bart's son Paul played the part of a writer and wine connoisseur named Miles in *Sideways*.

So Calvin Hill compared an 18-year-old Theo Epstein to Bart Giamatti, one of the most well-liked and respected men in the history of baseball.

It's safe to say Theo's future looked bright.

Of course Steinberg and Hill made sure that he got the job, and Theo began working as a summer intern for the Orioles in '92. A short while into his tenure, he wrote an extensive proposal and submitted it to Steinberg. Eloquently, Theo stated that the players and teams of the Negro Leagues had been underappreciated for too long. His suggestion was for the Orioles to honor the Negro Leagues, and do so as quickly as possible. Steinberg was flabbergasted by Theo's proposal; absolutely blown away. "As quickly as possible," didn't quite happen for Theo, but Steinberg instructed Baltimore's brass to follow Theo's lead. A year later, the Orioles paid tribute to the neglected African-American baseball superstars. The Orioles hosted the Major League Baseball All-Star Game that year, and during the festivities, Theo's project was one of the main attractions.

This was no average intern. Theo was making moves long before his days as general manager of the Boston Red Sox.

As word of Theo's thoughts and ideas traveled around the Orioles' organization, it stopped for a rest in Lucchino's ear. His Yale buddies Hill and Steinberg had mentioned Theo a number of times, and Lucchino grew increasingly more intrigued by the ambitious, young intern. Lucchino, too, developed a rapport with Theo, and it was easy for him to see the potential that Steinberg and Hill spoke of. But when majority owner Eli Jacobs auctioned away the Orioles after the 1993 season, Lucchino took his show on the road. He never quite had the time to groom Theo in Baltimore, but made note of the rising star. The two would meet again in the not too distant future.

Lucchino made his presence felt with the San Diego Padres in 1995. As the team's president and CEO, Lucchino started gathering coworkers he could trust. Not surprisingly, he put in a call to Steinberg. After very little persuasion, Steinberg agreed to join Lucchino in sunny San Diego. At that point, Theo had graduated from Yale. He wanted to continue his work in Major League Baseball, but knew it wouldn't be the same without Steinberg in Baltimore. Steinberg was his mentor—a man who certainly knew the ropes in baseball, and in life.

About 40 years earlier, Theo's father, Leslie, left the west coast for the east, transitioning from California to Connecticut. It was time for Theo to do the opposite; he packed up his things at Yale, went home to take care of a few things in Boston, and then took off for San Diego. He was on his way to his father's home state, without his father, or the rest of his family. It was a big move for a young man who didn't even have a driver's license. That's right, folks, Theo was 21 years old, and was incapable of driving himself around. Without his family and without legal permission to drive, Theo had a couple of things to figure out on his flight to California. One conclusion was inevitable: Steinberg would be his closest confidant.

With the Padres, Theo started in the entertainment department, putting birthday messages up on the Jumbotron and doing some low-level public relations work. Steinberg drove him to and from work everyday, and friends chauffeured Theo on the weekends. After grinding and paying his dues in the entertainment division for a year, he was promoted to a PR assistant spot, a position that required him to help with media guides and game notes, among other things.

"When Theo was in media relations I got to know him a little bit," said Padres' general manager Kevin Towers. "He had tremendous writing skills and a great interest in Baseball Operations. I think he was eager to somehow find a way to get more involved in that side of things."

Today a prideful man, ever aware of the magnitude of his accomplishments as Red Sox general manager, Theo hates talking about his errand running and order-taking with the Padres. He shudders at the memories of his pre-1997 professional days.

"I hated it," Theo told *New York Times* reporter Ginia Bellafante. "I don't like dealing with other peoples' problems. I like working on a common goal. I like a win or loss every day."

So why was '97 any different for Theo? Because that was the year Towers moved him into Baseball Operations.

"Everybody liked Theo," Towers said of the decision to move him up the ranks. "His personal skills were great and he seemed to fit in everywhere. There was no job too little for him or beneath him—whatever we wanted him to do, he'd roll up his sleeves and get it done."

"Theo was also the type of guy," Towers continued, "that could complete a project in 24 hours that would take a regular intern a few weeks."

If that wasn't enough of an indicator of Theo's potential, Towers received a rousing recommendation from Lucchino, who raved about his young protégé. Theo's decision to follow Steinberg out west was finally beginning to look like the right one.

Nineteen ninety-seven was also the year that Theo got his driver's license (congrats, Theo). He was a 23-year-old rookie on the road—a late bloomer, no doubt one that the scouts would overlook.

While Theo was making an impression in Baseball Operations, he was leading a bit of a double life. Theo was Clark Kent by day, but at night he was Superman at the University of San Diego School of Law. As a return for driving Theo around and helping him settle in San Diego, Steinberg virtually forced him to get a law degree.

Steinberg knew—in part from his friend Larry's success—that a degree in law made it easier to advance in the business world. He wanted Theo to reap the same benefits.

Theo obliged, though it was difficult for him to keep his mind off baseball. When the stamina was there, he would attend night class; when it wasn't, Theo traded Padres tickets to classmates in exchange for notes. He was always wheeling and dealing, no matter what the circumstances.

Theo may have missed class here and there, but wasn't missing any of the information. His spongy mind absorbed plenty of the law... enough to help him pass the California Bar Exam on his very first try. Jerry Brown, attorney general of California and former state governor, failed his bar the first time around. Hillary Clinton (Washington, D.C.) and John F. Kennedy, Jr. (New York) tanked their initial bars, as well. Hitting a home run with his first swing, there was no question that Theo had extensive knowledge of the law.

In lieu of his accomplishment, the Anaheim law firm of Gibson, Dunn & Crutcher came a-knockin'. Theo was making around $30,000 in Baseball Operations with the Padres. Put modestly, Gibson, Dunn & Crutcher were offering a bit more:

A cool $140,000 for his first year on the job.

It was a big number, but Theo's heart belonged to baseball. Emily Carhart, Gibson, Dunn & Crutcher's director of Communications, said no one at the firm seems to remember Theo today. He was a summer associate for a couple of months, but similar to his days in the Yale American Studies program, he didn't leave much of an impression. Theo's mind was always on baseball; he devoted virtually all of his energy and passion to the game, and his other endeavors got what was left of him.

Towers recalled Theo's short career in law.

"[Theo] had a great weekend with the guys at the firm, called me and said, 'K.T., these guys are fun, but baseball is in my blood. I want to be in baseball regardless of what the salary is.'"

Even so, Theo asked Towers for an increase in pay. He once called his original Padres' salary "embarrassing." He knew the Padres wouldn't match the law firm's offer—it just wasn't a realistic expectation—but when Towers responded a few days later with an offer, it was more than enough for Theo. He received a promotion and a nice boost in salary as the new Padres' director of Baseball Operations, making $80,000 a year.

Not long after taking over the baseball operational throne, Theo helped the Padres to one of their greatest seasons in franchise history. In 1995, while Theo was getting coffee for his coworkers and putting up, "Will you marry me, Lisa, my little honey pie?" on the Jumbotron, the Padres struggled. In what was a strike-shortened 144-game season, San Diego finished with an unimpressive 70-74 record. They were third in the National League Western Division, a division that, at the time, had only four teams.

(The Arizona Diamondbacks have since joined the fray.) The Padres were up in '96 (first place), and down in '97 (last place), but once Theo got settled in his high-ranking position, San Diego made the jump to the next level.

"Theo opened my eyes to better statistics like OPS, strikeout-to-walk ratio, and ballpark factors," Towers said. "I had more of a traditional scouting background; Theo was able to teach me the analytical side of things, and in turn I taught him how to pick up on key intangibles of players that don't show up in the statistics."

In Theo's first year in Baseball Operations he and Towers brought in Quilvio Veras and Greg Vaughn, two offensive starters that would play pivotal roles in '98, the Padres' breakout season. That year Vaughn hit 50 homers and drive in 119 runs, anchoring San Diego's lineup.

After the '97 debacle, Theo and Towers (let's call them "TNT") felt their team's pitching needed to be addressed. Enter Kevin Brown, a right-handed starting pitcher with nasty stuff and an even nastier attitude. Everywhere he went—Texas, Baltimore, and Florida before San Diego—he was regarded as a bit of a head case. Theo wondered if Brown's demeanor would affect his team's chemistry, but ultimately, the Padres needed an ace. Brown would be exactly that, going 18-7 with a 2.38 ERA and 257 strikeouts in '98.

TNT also added a couple of key right-handed relievers during the '07-08 off-season: Dan Miceli and Donne Wall. The previous year, lights-out closer Trevor Hoffman was San Diego's only regular reliever with an ERA under 4.77. For the Padres, Miceli went on to win 10 games out of the bullpen with a 3.22 ERA, and Wall posted a pretty 2.43 ERA in over 70 innings of work.

What did all of the moves add up to? The 1998 San Diego Padres defeated the all-powerful Atlanta Braves to become the champions of the National League. It was only the second trip to the World Series for the Padres, and Theo was an essential off-the-field contributor to their success.

The three amigos—Theo, Steinberg, and Lucchino— had left their imprint on the Padres' franchise. In San Diego, Theo and Lucchino had grown closer than they were in Baltimore. Lucchino became privy to Theo's exceptional talents.

A few years later, Lucchino shipped off to Boston. Owner John Harrington put the Red Sox up for sale, and Lucchino quickly called John W. Henry. Henry was the owner of "JWH," John W. Henry & Company, Inc., an alternative asset manager founded in 1982. JWH manages assets for "retail, institutional and private investors in the Americas, Europe and Asia," according to the company website. When Lucchino called Henry, business was booming at JWH.

Lucchino wanted Henry to team up with Tom Werner, an extremely wealthy TV producer, to buy the Red Sox, but there were a few problems: (1) Henry was already the owner of the Florida Marlins, and (2) if he escaped

Florida, he was going to pursue the Anaheim Angels. But it was no secret that Major League Baseball commissioner Bud Selig wanted the lovable Red Sox in good hands, so he made sure of a buyer for Henry's Marlins. Lucchino got Henry's mind off California, and before everyone knew it, Henry and Werner were in control of the Red Sox.

In the meantime, Theo spent another year in the Padres' front office. During the season Blue Jays' general manager J.P. Ricciardi made his interest in Theo known. Ricciardi wanted Theo to join Toronto's staff as his right-hand man and assistant GM. Theo was flattered, but had to decline for the time being.

"Theo and I had nightly discussions about J.P.'s offer of the assistant general manager position," Towers said. "But Theo had just as good a chance to get a GM offer working with us as he would have in Toronto. Ultimately, he said, 'My dream job is to work for the Red Sox.'"

Theo was straight with Ricciardi: he told him that he was waiting on a call from Boston.

At year's end, the phone rang. It was Lucchino—like Ricciardi, he offered Theo the position of assistant to the general manager. GM Dan Duquette had been fired, and Mike Port was penciled in as the interim, so it was an excellent opportunity for Theo. There was a sense that Port was a lame duck, leaving the door open for the future. Theo was ready to go.

Not so fast, said Padres' owner John Moores. Moores was quite aware of Theo's reputation and potential, and he wasn't obligated to let him walk. For a while, Moores refused to let Lucchino negotiate officially. But Moores was told that Theo would be back at home in Boston, so out of courtesy he eventually granted the Red Sox 48 hours to negotiate.

"Did we want to lose Theo? No, absolutely not," Towers said. "But how do you stand in the way of a kid who has a chance to go home and run such a storied franchise?"

Clearly, the 48-hour window was more than enough time. Theo said so long to the sun, and returned to the wild New England weather. Steinberg would be in Boston with him, as well.

Theo Epstein was back with his family, teamed up with his friends (Lucchino and Steinberg), and working in the front office of the Boston Red Sox, the team he lived and died for as a kid. Life was good. It didn't seem like it could get any better…

But it did. Port held the title of interim general manager when Theo arrived, but according to people inside the organization, his title was merely for show.

"Theo was essentially doing the GM's job," said Voros McCracken, a special consultant to Baseball Operations for the Red Sox from October 2002 to June 2005. "Mike [Port] was basically a business front. Theo did the bulk of the work in Baseball Operations."

Lucchino planned to go after a big-name GM during the off-season, but just in case, Theo was being groomed. When the '02 season came to a close, Lucchino went to work.

His target was Billy Beane, the Oakland Athletics' outstanding general manager. Beane, a former big-time MLB prospect, had turned nothing into something in Oakland. The Athletics' payroll was laughably low, and yet Beane put together a roster that won him an American League Western Division title in 2000. He knew the immense value of walks, OBP, and slugging percentage—three stats that Theo swore by. Theo approved of Beane, and would do everything he could to help Lucchino get his man.

Late in November, Theo and Lucchino hooked Beane with a record offer: a five-year deal worth $12.5 million. The contract was going to make Beane the highest paid GM in major league history, but to Theo, Lucchino, and Henry, it would have been money well spent.

"Would have been," because at the last minute, Beane backed out of the deal. He didn't want to leave his wife, Tara, and 13-year-old daughter, Casey. He didn't want to leave his young pitching staff, either.

"For 24 hours, to think I took the choice not to have [Tim] Hudson, [Mark] Mulder and [Barry] Zito... that's a fool," Beane said at a press conference.

Clearly Theo and Lucchino understood Beane's decision, but "Mr. Moneyball" left them in a tight spot. The off-season was progressing, and the Red Sox didn't have anyone to call the shots. Theo flipped the script on Ricciardi, and asked him to take over in Boston. But J.P. liked it up in Canada; his situation was comfortable, and he wasn't interested in the Red Sox's opening. (Hindsight is 20/20.)

Theo and Lucchino had no choice but to scratch their top two options off the list. The problem was, essentially, Beane and Ricciardi *were* the list. There were a few backdoor options, but Lucchino had to decide if they were worth it. Did it make sense for him to bring in a little-known outsider?

Ultimately, the answer was "no." Theo had been training throughout the '02 season, and Lucchino decided that it was time to make him the youngest general manager in the history of Major League Baseball. It was an overwhelming turn of events, but Theo wanted the job. His beautiful life became even more attractive. Besides, "He had been doing the job for an entire season anyway," according to McCracken.

On November 25, 2002, the Red Sox made it official.

"I know Billy [Beane] was our first choice," Lucchino told *New York Times* reporter Murray Chass, "but we feel pretty good that Theo is the right choice for the direction we want to go with the franchise. You can have more than one good choice. Theo has a lot of attributes we were looking for."

"We feel pretty good" is not exactly a screaming endorsement. Lucchino seemed a little unsure about Theo, even publicly, and there were rumblings of a showcase hiring.

"Larry, in a sense, wants to be the general manager but not be the general manager," a baseball official told *The Times.*

It sounded a little like Theo was working as general manager while Port held the title. However, Theo wasn't buying the media's spin on his working relationship with Lucchino.

"I laugh at people who call me sort of a yes-man for Larry or who claim that I'm beholden to Larry in any way," he said. "I wish they could see some of our discussions. We really go at it."

And they would again in the future, but the discussions would escalate to arguments—heated ones. But that was the future. In the present, no one knew how the front office situation would shake out. All Theo knew was that he was excited about his new position.

"It's a difficult task, but it's not mission impossible," Theo said. "We have such a common bond with the fan: we all want to win so badly, we have shared experiences. It's a thrill to be able to change that."

And he would.

Methods, Strategies... Secrets?

From the minute the promotion to general manager was made official, baseball insiders were buzzing about Theo. Everyone seemed to agree that he was a "smart kid," but was that enough to create faith in his ability to command a Major League Baseball roster?

There had to be more. In Baltimore, Steinberg, Hill, and Lucchino had to see more than just a young man who was familiar with baseball's history and could articulate his thoughts well. In San Diego, there had to be a reason why GM Kevin Towers upped Theo's salary by about $50,000 when he thought he might lose him to the Gibson, Dunn & Crutcher law firm. Lucchino must have known there was something special about Theo when he fought vigorously to snatch him away from the Padres, and bring him home to Boston. The question is—what was it? What told everyone that Theo could be an impact front office player?

Everything. In Bill Lajoie's first couple of months on

the job, he watched Theo very closely. Lajoie (pronounced la-joy), then the Red Sox's 69-year-old assistant to the general manager, had been in baseball since the '50s. Having worked as the GM of the Detroit Tigers in the past, he knew what to look for in Theo. He got a feel for the young executive's personality, demeanor, smarts, and ability to interact with people in all areas of Major League Baseball. It wasn't long before Lajoie felt the need to pull Theo aside, and give him a potentially life-altering piece of advice.

"Theo, you should be in baseball no longer than 10 years," Lajoie said sternly.

Perhaps he saw that Theo was unfit for his job. Had the Red Sox made a terrible mistake in naming Theo the youngest GM in the history of baseball?

Not exactly. Lajoie looked Theo in the eyes and continued.

"You have an extraordinary gift to help people in the United States," Lajoie told his young counterpart. "You should run for senator, and eventually run for president. You are the type of person who can handle it."

No laugh followed; Lajoie was not kidding. In front of him stood a 29-year-old man, one who fans and media members commonly referred to as a "boy" or "kid," but Lajoie knew better. Theo Epstein was a polished, personable professional that could make a difference in the world.

However, Towers wouldn't second Lajoie's notion, nor

would Craig Shipley, the Red Sox's vice president of International Scouting. "I have some skeletons still in Theo's closet," Towers chuckled. "Let's just say I can't quite see him running the country."

"President of the United States?" Shipley asked rhetorically. "I don't know about that."

All right, maybe the presidency's a long shot. But even before his days in Boston, Theo was building a reputation as one of the hardest workers in baseball. After Towers moved him into Baseball Operations in San Diego, Theo never once took his great opportunity for granted. He wanted his presence to be felt; he didn't want to be a quiet contributor or a run-of-the-mill stat guy, so he worked to become as close to irreplaceable as possible. During the off-season most of the Padres' decision-makers would head home around 5:30 or 6 p.m.; Lucchino would be in his office until 8 or 9. When he was ready to pack things up for the evening, there would be one coworker left on the floor: Theo. He'd be in his quadrant late working on various projects, conducting research, analysis, and doing projections.

One of those projects was a study of the pecking order of major league prospects. Learn a few names from each organization, get an idea of their strengths and weaknesses—in theory, it seemed like an easy enough task. Only Theo didn't learn the top two or three names; he memorized every team's *entire* depth chart, from top to bottom. Lucchino would not soon forget Theo's work ethic.

Still, there were plenty of young, smart, hard workers out there. Was that all it took for Theo to be named director of Baseball Operations in San Diego, and assistant general manager upon his return to Beantown?

Not quite. Theo wasn't just "smart"; he was one of *the* most impressive, intelligent, intellectual, intriguing, engaging, capable, and versatile young men that the Red Sox's seasoned baseball professionals had ever known, or heard of, for that matter.

Lucchino once asked Lajoie, "How often does an individual like Theo come around?"

"Once in 10 million," Lajoie said.

Lucchino upped the ante. "More like once in a hundred million," he responded.

Touché. The Red Sox's upper management knew they had a special person in Theo Epstein, the kind of person that could do wonders in the baseball world but had the mind, ability, and personality to succeed at anything, anywhere.

Theo's knowledge of Bill James' sophisticated baseball theories and strategies also set him apart from the pack. Billy Beane had taken some of James' work into account while implementing his *Moneyball* strategies in Oakland and his ideology certainly seemed to generate success. Theo hoped to do the same in Boston, but wasn't about to leave things up to chance. Late in 2002, the Red Sox hired James as senior advisor to Baseball Operations. Theo would have an extremely valuable asset at his side as his general managerial reign began.

Theo was of the strategic minority: those in baseball who read James, and actually decided to implement some of his ideas. Starting from the very basic, Theo planned to eliminate the sacrifice bunt from Boston's offense, with very rare exceptions. The sacrifice bunt is used to move a runner or runners into scoring position with zero or one out. The batter squares around early and gives himself up, dropping a bunt down the first or third base side depending on the position of the runners.

Theo felt the sacrifice bunt was a dated strategic maneuver, and that it was an unproductive use of an out. He believed it to be an illogical play because after a sac is laid down, the runners are left on second and/or third base with one or two outs. The problem is that the league-wide batting average with runners in scoring position is significantly lower than the regular league average. Strategically, it didn't make sense to give away an out and hope that one of the following batters would defy the numbers. It was more efficient to retain the outs and allow the opportunity for a walk, a hit-by-pitch, an extra-base hit, back-to-back singles or anything else that wouldn't constitute a surrendered out.

More importantly, Theo viewed the sacrifice bunt as a rally killer. If a hitter leads off an inning with a solid single, bunting him over with the next batter lets the opposing pitcher off the hook. The first out of an inning can be elusive at times, and handing it to the other team on a silver platter represented sub-optimal offensive philosophy. James placed the sac bunt in the category of "one-run strategies." That meant exactly what it sounded like: the team using the strategy was playing to score once as opposed to going for the kill, and piling up runs. In general, one-run strategies weren't very appealing to Theo or James.

Also, Theo was aware that the sac bunt was far from a sure thing. All of the following could go wrong: (1) the hitter completely misses the bunt, giving away a strike; (2) the hitter fouls off the bunt, with the same result; (3) the hitter strikes out bunting a two-strike pitch into foul territory; (4) the hitter bunts the ball hard to the first or third baseman, allowing them the time to cut down the lead runner instead of taking the sure out at first; (5) the hitter pops up the bunt and gets the runner doubled off first or second base; (6) the hitter bunts the ball hard back to the pitcher, inducing a 1-6-3 double play; or (7) the runner gets a head start toward the next base to eliminate the possibility of a force out, and the hitter misses the bunt, allowing the catcher to throw behind the runner and trap him in a rundown.

Also, Fenway Park is widely regarded as one of the elite hitters' parks. Giving away an out is ill advised when the Green Monster can turn a routine 310-foot fly ball into a stand-up double. In right field, the Pesky Pole area is favorable to left-handed hitters, as well.

*Fenway Park, a hitter's park where 'routine outs'
can be routine doubles, or more*

Clearly there were many reasons for Theo to dismiss the sac bunt. Since the Red Sox are an American League team, it wasn't hard for Theo to sell the idea to his constituents. Typically the sacrifice bunt is more of a necessity in the National League, where the pitcher has to bat.

Theo identified similar problems with the stolen base. In his intense research, James found that teams who lead the majors in stolen bases rarely ever reach the World Series, let alone win it. When used correctly with the right runner on the base paths, and a pitcher who is slow to the plate and/or lacks a strong pick-off move, the stolen base can be a weapon. But Theo recognized that teams overused that weapon, often forcing the action and running themselves out of innings. He didn't want to ignore the stolen base; he merely wanted the Red Sox to be more cautious with their use of it.

Another fundamental problem with the stolen base is that the fastest runners on a team often bat in front of the premier hitters. So when a speedy guy gets thrown out trying to get himself into scoring position with two outs, he takes the bat out of the hands of the No. 3 or 4 hitter, forcing the big bopper to lead off the next inning with no one on base. That middle of the order guy could have produced an extra-base hit that would have scored the runner from first, anyway. In a second scenario, the 3-hitter could single, pushing the burner into scoring position for the No. 4 man, opening up the possibility for a three-run homer.

The hit-and-run play didn't make much sense to Theo, either. On a hit-and-run, the runner on first takes off for second as the pitcher is delivering to home plate. The batter is *obligated* to swing; it doesn't matter if the pitch is a ball. In anticipation of funny business, the opposing manager can call for a pitch out, and even when that happens, the batter involved in the hit-and-run is supposed to throw his bat at the ball to protect his runner from being caught stealing. Why is he protecting his runner at all costs? Because the runner is not attempting a "straight steal." A straight steal is when the runner tries to get a huge jump and looks only at second base as the pitch is thrown. In a hit-and-run situation, the runner gets a modest jump and looks back at home plate to pick up the flight of the ball.

Like the sacrifice bunt, Theo identified a number of things that could go wrong with a hit-and-run. To name some: (1) the batter misses the sign from the third base coach, takes the pitch, and leaves his runner out to dry in the middle of first and second base; (2) the runner misses the sign, stays put, and costs the batter a strike as he swings at a pitch way off the plate; (3) the batter swings and misses, and gets the runner thrown out at second; or (4) the batter hits a line drive directly at an infielder, resulting in a virtually automatic double-play.

Also, corner outfielders tend to play in at Fenway Park. The objective for a hitter involved in a hit-and-run is to stroke a line drive behind the runner into the hole vacated by the fielder sprinting to cover second base. If the hitter gets a little loft into their line drive, the right fielder may be shallow enough to catch it and then double the runner off first.

Theo's concerns about the sacrifice bunt, the stolen base, and the hit-and-run play were legitimate. He was particularly against the sac bunt and hit-and-run, and wanted all members of the Red Sox's organization—from the suits to the players—to be of a similar mindset.

Those were Theo's essential on-field strategies, all of which centered on the idea of placing greater value on each and every out. He wanted his Red Sox to give nothing away—and they wouldn't.

As far as off-the-field strategies—front office ideology—Theo had a message for his scouting department:

search for players who get on base. It seemed like a simple enough idea, but so many other organizations were blinded by players who looked the part with great size and raw power. Power is nice, and Theo certainly wasn't against players who could knock the cover off the ball, but he wanted smart run producers; run producers who would work the count in their favor, and take a walk when necessary. Theo's favorite stats are on-base percentage (OBP) and slugging percentage. When added together they equal a player's OPS; the higher the OPS, the more productive the player. Theo values OPS more than home runs or RBI.

In doing so, Theo has earned the "sabermetrician" label. According to James, the mad scientist who coined the term, "sabermetrics" is "the search for new knowledge about baseball; the systematic study of baseball questions." But inside baseball, the sabermetricians are identified as those who equated OPS with the crown jewel of statistics. Beane is considered a sabermetrician, as are J.P. Ricciardi in Toronto, Brian Sabean in San Francisco, and Paul DePodesta in Los Angeles (before he was fired). Theo's name is now firmly cemented on that list, though Lajoie says he differentiates himself from the pack.

"Theo takes things a step further than J.P. and Billy," Lajoie said. "He doesn't just use statistical information; he listens to his evaluators and people who make judgments about players. He considers the human element that can't be measured mathematically."

Theo also planned to construct a player evaluation team that covered all the analytical bases. In James, he had the elite and most creative statistician in the game. James could provide a perspective unparalleled by other stat men around the league, with unique tools like win shares, runs produced, secondary average, and the defensive spectrum. Jamesian theory can be a bit controversial at times—often he has said, "There is no such thing as a clutch hitter"—but ultimately there is no one more diligent and thorough in his field. Theo agreed with many of James' ideas and theories, which made it easy for the duo to communicate and assess potential transactions from all statistical angles.

Theo recently spoke about James' contributions to the Red Sox.

"I know with Bill that I'm always going to get a unique perspective," Theo said earlier this year in a *60 Minutes* interview. "I think he does see the game from a different vantage point of almost anyone else. His basic questions about the game have allowed us to think more critically about the best way to develop players. Even if he doesn't have the answers, he always has the questions."

Elsewhere in the front office, in Ben Cherington (now vice president of Player Personnel) Theo inherited a sharp, young mind that had experience as an advanced scout with the Cleveland Indians. The two were very close in age, and thus, on a similar cognitive wavelength. Cherington was a "Duquette guy," but Theo kept him around because of his youth and incredible long-term potential. Cherington had the versatility to provide sophisticated evaluations of a player's statistics *and* physical skills, making his value to the club undeniable.

The man forever tied to Cherington, Jed Hoyer, was another invaluable member of Theo's gang. (Cherington and Hoyer were named co-general managers during Theo's future hiatus). Hoyer graduated from Wesleyan University, a fine academic school, and left his mark on the baseball program as the all-time saves leader. Also young and brilliant like Theo and Cherington, Hoyer could provide the perspective of both a ballplayer and executive. Today, he's the Red Sox's assistant general manager.

In scouting, Theo had true "baseball guys" in Lajoie and Craig Shipley. Shipley spent parts of 11 years in the major leagues, combining time with the Los Angeles Dodgers, New York Mets, San Diego Padres, Houston Astros, and Anaheim Angels. He is often remembered as a Padre because he played four seasons in San Diego, "shipped" off to Houston, and then returned to the Padres for two more years. Shipley was the prototypical utility man, a middle infielder with the ability to play third base and a little outfield if necessary. He failed to find offensive consistency, and as a result, never logged more than 240 at bats in a single season.

As a player, Shipley was far from an All-Star, but as a scout, he had the knowledge and first-hand experience necessary to become a superstar. He was always a cerebral player, an extension of the manager on the field and in the clubhouse, and one could argue that his baseball awareness—not his physical talent—is what kept him at the major league level. In addition, his defensive versatility made it easy for him to effectively evaluate mechanics at multiple positions.

Shipley was in baseball ops with the Montreal Expos and San Diego Padres before signing on with Theo shortly after he took command. With the Red Sox, Shipley has worked as a special assistant to the GM, and ran both professional and international scouting in '06 and '07. He is currently vice president of International Scouting.

Lajoie, now 74 years old, had the most experience of the bunch, both in baseball and life itself. He played ball at Western Michigan University, and was a first-team All-American back in 1955. Lajoie started his professional career with the Baltimore Orioles, and was a minor leaguer through 1964. Along the way, he enjoyed cups of coffee with five different big league clubs.

Following his playing days, Lajoie worked as an area scout and cross-checker before climbing the ladder to scouting director of the Detroit Tigers in 1974. From there he became the club's farm director and vice president of Player Personnel en route to a promotion in 1983. From '83 till '90, Lajoie ran the show as general manager of the Tigers. He has two claims to fame from that time period: (1) he was the man who traded a young John Smoltz for an aging Doyle Alexander. Smoltz went on to become one of the greatest and most versatile pitchers in the history of the major leagues, and to this day, Lajoie's move rests comfortably near the top of every "Worst Trades" list. ESPN's *Sportscenter* seems to mention the deal annually at the trade deadline.

And (2) on the flip side, Lajoie led the Tigers to a World Series title in 1984. After his days in Detroit, he provided his services as a special consultant to the Atlanta Braves, and then the Milwaukee Brewers. Lajoie's run with the Red Sox began in November of 2003, and concluded with his resignation in January of 2006. Near the end of his tenure in Boston, he was thrust in the middle of an undesirably sticky situation. Foreseeing a future of conflict and division, Lajoie left the kitchen before the smoke detector went off. (More on the "sticky situation" later.)

Still, Lajoie is among the most vehement of all Theo endorsers.

"He's one of the finest young men I've ever met," Lajoie said of Theo. "He may, in fact, be the finest. You won't hear anyone in the Red Sox's organization say one bad word about him."

With Lajoie's invaluable experience added to the mix, Theo's dream team was fully assembled. His on and off-field strategies went hand-in-hand—load up the front office with good eyes for talent, and bolster the roster with "good eyes" at the plate.

Strategically, Theo wanted to get his players on base in any possible fashion, and score runs without donating outs to the opposition. It was a style more generally known as "station-to-station" baseball. "Station-to-station" meant walks and hits would determine his team's fate. Like a merry-go-round, consecutive walks and hits can move runners fluidly around the bases. Theo's baseball philosophy was appropriate for the American League, particularly for a team in the Eastern Division, the home of the always-powerful Yankees. His strategy turned every inning into a potential rally, and gave the Red Sox the chance to become one of the most prolific offensive clubs in baseball.

Theo also needed a policy on free agency. The Red Sox are a big market organization, which meant Theo would have mountains of cash at his disposal. Wisely, he didn't plan to max out his credit card; he wanted his club to build its minor league system and promote players from the inside before taking hacks at high-priced free agents. From the very beginning, Theo was looking ahead.

"Never prioritize one year over the future," said Theo of his farm system in an interview with Yahoo Sports. "[We] start planning for a season three or four years in advance; the decisions you make over the course of a long period effect the upcoming season."

Theo didn't shun free agency—not by any means—but similar to his philosophy about the stolen base, he wanted the Red Sox to use the weapon properly. Instead of firing wildly and emptying an entire clip, he wanted to take accurate, measured shots on the open market. Theo knew he could make friends with free agency at the right time, for the right player, and at the right price.

As far as pitching went, like many other execs around the league, Theo had a thing for power arms. The basic thought is this: you can teach a hard thrower how to pitch, but you can't teach a pitcher who throws 88 mph how to throw 98. Theo wanted his scouts to pursue the pitchers with the most natural ability, and for his player development guys to refine those pitchers.

Drafting power arms also allows for a more durable pitching staff. When hurlers who throw 96 to 99 mph suffer through an inevitable "dead arm" period during the long season, their fastball remains effective in the 92-to-94 range. But when a finesse pitcher who tops out at 90 begins to tire, their "heater" becomes an "er." The heat disappears and they're left with an 85-to-87 mph fastball (if it can still be called that), the type that major league hitters drive deep into the night. The common misnomer is that a finesse pitcher can fall back on their off-speed stuff; not true, even junkballers need a decent fastball in order to keep hitters from sitting on one speed.

In addition, power arms have a better shot at successful longevity. Control pitchers can stick around for a long time, but they can't maintain the All-Star level of their younger days. Think Greg Maddux. "The Bulldog" has been able to pitch in the big leagues for over 20 years, but hasn't been to the Midsummer Classic as a senior citizen. It's been eight seasons since Maddux's last trip to the

All-Star Game; that in comparison to power pitchers like John Smoltz, Roger Clemens, and Curt Schilling, who remained among the league's elite in their old age.

Theo knew that power arms were the way to go, and Red Sox fans would see their fare share of them in the coming years: Jonathan Papelbon, Jon Lester, Craig Hansen, and Clay Buchholz, to name some. Flamethrowers don't always pan out but are the savviest long-term investment. Those who can't hack it as starters can still become very successful relievers.

Statistically, while most other teams were gazing at pitchers' won-lost records, Theo and James were taking a good, hard look at strikeout-to-walk ratios, as well as ballpark effects.

With hard throwers, smart hitters, and conservative offensive baseball, Theo had covered most of the ideological bases. But one was missing: how would he interact with his players, staff members, and those of other organizations?

"You sit in a [contract] meeting with him," Lajoie said of Theo, "and he handles four agents as if they are one. He has an amazing wherewithal as to his surroundings and commanding the respect of the room. He's a force."

That's not all.

"It doesn't matter if it's talking to agents, other GMs, his own personnel, or as far down the chain as area scouts," Lajoie continued, "[Theo] has a natural rapport with people at all levels within the organization."

Even the men on the field. Before making a decision about a draft pick or signing, Theo likes to get to know the players. When the opportunity presents itself, he meets with them personally to get a feel for their disposition and attitude for the game. If a meeting can't be arranged, Theo or members of his staff call the player's previous organization and request a character evaluation, a procedure that paid incredible dividends in his original assessment of David Ortiz (see chapter 5).

Theo considers attitudes and personalities because he wants his players to gel, and avoid unnecessary friction with teammates. After working as the Red Sox's unofficial GM in 2002, he had a tight grasp on the personality of his ball club, and knew what worked and didn't work about his team's dynamic. Theo's thoroughness in player evaluation could have been construed as a hands-on approach to dealing with players, and in a way, it was. But once his 25-man roster was set, he would back off a great deal. His method seemed just right.

"I like to be around enough to be accountable and available, but the clubhouse is the player's sanctuary," Theo has said. "It's their place to get away from things."

With that philosophy, it was easy for Theo to gain the respect of his players. In the future, the world would see how much his players liked him... as they partied and sprayed him with champagne after the World Series victories of 2004 and 2007.

Theo values OPS and walks like Billy Beane, but visibility is one area in which he differs from Oakland's architect. Theo likes to let his players do their own thing in the clubhouse, whereas Beane is constantly around his players. Beane asks his players questions to get a feel for their physical and mental make-up at different points in the season, whereas Theo lets his guys work things out internally, or with the appropriate member of his coaching staff. No matter what the circumstances of the season, Theo never exudes the impression that he is panicking. As a result, his players feel that their employers have confidence in them.

When it comes to the 150 to 200 people working below him in the front office, Theo values the most dedicated. He prefers workers who fulfill the requirements of their position and do so with one common goal in mind: getting to the postseason every year. It's not that he's against ambition—of course, Theo was ambitious in his progression from a Baltimore Orioles' intern to the Red Sox's general manager—but he wants his inferiors to pay their dues before actively seeking a promotion. Understandably, he doesn't like when a person comes in at the entry-level and expects to be director of Baseball Operations within a year.

Theo makes all of his workers feel as if their opinion is valued, even interns. A former high-ranking Red Sox official said he walked out of player meetings when Theo allowed interns to attend. "Player meetings" are held to discuss possible additions, often around the trade deadline. The Red Sox official disapproved of intern participation because it was difficult to trust them with confidential information. What happened in player meetings, was supposed to stay in player meetings—sort of like the first rule of *Fight Club*.

Not only did the interns get to listen to the top-secret, behind-the-scenes discussions... they were given the opportunity to *contribute*. Theo often asked interns for their opinions about players and potential transactions.

Back in 2003, one intern voiced his displeasure with starting pitcher Jeff Suppan, then of the Pittsburgh Pirates. He didn't like Suppan's stuff or arm action, and was frankly appalled by the right-hander's inclusion in the discussion. Regardless, on July 31, Theo traded infield prospect Freddy Sanchez to Pittsburgh for Suppan, who had already pitched for Boston from '95 to '97.

Suppan proceeded to get rocked in his return to a Red Sock uniform. Going 3-4 with a 5.57 ERA, Suppan was a bust. Sanchez went on to win the National League batting title in 2006, with a .344 average.

Theo should have listened to his young employee.

But in those instances, it was the thought that counted. People love working under Theo because he makes everyone feel as if they are important to the organization, and that their efforts can make an impact.

With that, Theo's recipe for success is complete: value talented, focused and dedicated staff members, build a farm system and roster jam-packed with heady hitters and explosive pitchers, work to ensure an acceptable level of team chemistry, be accountable but not overbearing with the players, and once you get out there on the field, hold on to each and every out for dear life.

Give nothing away.

Except "Boston Red Sox World Series champion" T-shirts at the victory parade.

Reviving a Franchise

The Theo Epstein era began officially on November 25, 2002, when "The Wonder Boy" was named general manager of the Boston Red Sox. Theo, then just 28 years old, earned the incredible distinction of the youngest GM in Major League Baseball history.

"We're going to become a championship organization," said Theo, confidently, at his introductory press conference. "We're going to win a World Series."

The local papers weren't quite as confident. With headlines like "The Rookie," "Boston Bids Kid Hello," and "Boston Picks a Wonder Boy," it sounded like the Sox had hired an elementary school kid to run the show. The media presented Theo as the Doogie Howser of the baseball world.

Red Sox fans rolled their eyes at the time of Theo's bold statement, but this "kid" was not joking. Everyone would soon learn to take him seriously.

In the previous decade, the hated New York Yankees

had made Brian Cashman the youngest general manager of all time. It seemed to work out OK—Cashman started in 1998 and the Yankees won the World Series in '98, '99, and 2000. Not bad.

Of course Red Sox's principal owner John Henry and president/CEO Larry Lucchino weren't looking to follow in the rival Yankees' footsteps, but at least they knew they weren't dipping into uncharted waters. Cashman was only two years older than Theo when his reign with the Yankees began.

Theo was regarded by many as one of the sharpest, most innovative young minds in the game. Theo's predecessor, Mike Port, was a respected baseball man, but Lucchino didn't project him as a long-term general managerial solution. It was the right time to bring Theo into the fold because Boston's roster boasted a few crown jewels, and Theo would have plenty of Henry's money to play around with. The front office trusted Theo, but the fluffy cushion provided by Henry and the roster holdovers made his success all the more feasible.

"Irrespective of his age, we are confident Theo is among the best and the brightest in baseball," said Red Sox chairman Tom Werner. "We believe that the team he'll assemble will achieve results for which we so yearn."

Werner was right; but fortunately for Theo, he wouldn't have to assemble *all* of the key pieces. Some were already in place.

The 2002 Red Sox were no joke. They had finished 24 games over the .500 mark (93-69), and fell just short of the Anaheim Angels, the eventual World Series champions, in the American League Wild Card race. Theo would inherit an excellent core including positioned players Jason Varitek, Johnny Damon, and Trot Nixon, and pitchers Derek Lowe and Tim Wakefield.

Oh, there were a few other decent players, too: franchise shortstop Nomar Garciaparra, a Fenway faithful favorite, one of the most prolific offensive shortstops of all time; zany left fielder Manny Ramirez, a purely natural hitter, arguably the premier run producer in baseball, and Pedro Martinez, the league's most intimidating and effective starting pitcher.

"Manny being Manny" before it sent him on his way

It was a three-headed monster that put a spook into the opposition and a smile on Theo's face. All three were under contract for the 2003 season, so Theo was free to devote his energy elsewhere. He could have easily been conservative with that energy, filling in the vacated spots with role players and letting his stars do the work in 2003, but Theo intended to unleash his baseball philosophy on the world. He may have been new to the job, but he was not averse to taking risks. Theo's very first off-season would prove to be the gutsiest and most controversial of his career to date.

Theo's decision that started the ball rolling toward innovation was the one to let closer Ugueth Urbina go. Urbina was superb in 2002, striking out 71 in 60 innings of work, while posting a 3.00 ERA en route to 40 saves. Theo allowed Urbina to venture into the lucrative waters of free agency, and the hard-throwing right-hander washed up on shore with the Texas Rangers. Theo was then without a closer, and wasn't the least bit concerned.

Theo had long been a student of his Senior Baseball Advisor Bill James, a master of statistics and strong proponent of sabermetrics. In *Baseball Abstracts*, he talked at length about bullpen management and construction. James believed that every bullpen would benefit from the presence of a dominant, standout reliever—what he called a "relief ace." No big deal there, that's a closer, right?

Not exactly. James didn't believe in the traditional closer's role. If a team had a lights-out reliever, James felt he should be used in each game's most critical situation, which in his mind, did not have to be the ninth inning with a lead of three runs or less. It could be the sixth inning with bases loaded in a tie game, or the eighth inning, trailing by a run and needing to hold the one-run deficit in order to have a chance against the other team's closer in the ninth. James' logic was certainly justifiable, and his theories were always in the back of Theo's mind.

With Urbina out of the picture, the Sox didn't have anyone they could trust in the closer's spot. None of Theo's relievers could even be considered a "relief ace." Considering the circumstances, Theo decided to turn to another of James' ideas: the interchangeable parts bullpen. In this system, a team's relief core would consist of six to eight pitchers of virtually equal ability. There would be no closer. Instead, the manager would be relied upon to make situational decisions depending upon righty-lefty match-ups, the circumstances of the inning, the runners on base, etc. For Theo, Grady Little would be the man trusted to make all of the moves. Little was a little skeptical of the experiment, but willing to give it a fair chance.

Regardless, Theo went to work piecing together his new-look bullpen. He brought in five right-handers: the reliable Ramiro Mendoza from the Yankees, the oft-injured but electric Chad Fox from the Brewers, young sinker-baller Brandon Lyon from the Blue Jays, hard-throwing journeyman Mike Timlin—formerly of the Phillies, Cardinals, Orioles, Mariners, and Blue Jays—and once decent Brewers' starter Steve Woodard, most recently a Texas Ranger.

The holdovers from the '02 bullpen were righty Bobby Howry and lefty Alan Embree. Both featured excellent fastballs; Howry's second pitch was a sharp curveball while Embree threw a sometimes-devastating splitter.

Right from the get-go, there was a potentially deadly chink in the armor of Boston's bullpen experiment: the relievers were supposed to be of equal ability and/or value, and that just wasn't the case with Theo's group. Lyon was unproven, heading into just his third major league season after pitching to a stomach turning 6.53 ERA the previous year. Woodard was straight off the scrap heap, a guy with mediocre stuff whose ERA was over 5.00 for five consecutive years leading up to the 2003 season.

There was no question that Lyon and Woodard deserved to be at the bottom of the Red Sox's bullpen totem poll. But there wasn't supposed to be a totem poll—"top" and "bottom" weren't supposed to exist—Theo's plan was for all of the relievers to be on the same plain.

The other five—Mendoza, Timlin, Fox, Embree, and Howry—were all veterans who had performed well in at least two full seasons in the past. Embree and Timlin both thrived in 2002, posting ERAs under 3.00; that fact combined with their explosive fastballs and general reliability, had to separate them from the pack.

In addition, there was no question that Fox had the best stuff of the bunch. With a plus fastball and a ridiculously nasty slider, most speculated that Fox would get the ball when a save opportunity presented itself (if he was still available).

With Fox, Embree, and Timlin near the top, Woodard and Lyon at the bottom, and Mendoza and Howry somewhere in between, there certainly appeared to be a hierarchy in Theo's "interchangeable" bullpen. It was an experiment doomed from the outset, and yet no one in the Red Sox organization stopped Theo from going through with it.

Growing pains, my friends… growing pains.

"After the first game in Tampa that season," said Bill Lajoie, then Boston's assistant to the general manager, "I remember going to Grady the next day and saying, 'Tell this man you want a closer.' He said, 'Oh no, Bill. I think we can work this out.'"

Little—the true gentleman that he is—was optimistic. Unfortunately, he was also wrong. They couldn't work it out.

With his club struggling mightily in the early going, Theo quickly realized his miscalculation, and began dismantling the pen project in the second month of the season. On May 29, 2003, he traded third baseman Shea Hillenbrand to the Arizona Diamondbacks for enigmatic reliever/starter Byung-Hyun Kim.

Kim was a unique pitcher, a side-winding righty who could freely toss his heater in the 91-to-93 mph range. As a generality, side-armers and side-winders are valued for their unorthodox arm angle, not for their velocity. Kim represented the best of both worlds, deceiving right-handed hitters with his arm slot, and using his hard, sinking fastball to his advantage against lefties.

As a closer, Kim's confidence had been shaken by the relentless Yankee lineup in the 2001 playoffs, but he bounced back beautifully in '02, saving 36 games and flaunting a minute 2.04 ERA. Kim had always preferred to be a starting pitcher, and the Diamondbacks rewarded him for his success in '02 by moving him into the rotation in '03. Prior to the trade Kim struggled to find a way to win as a starter, going 1-5, but his 3.56 ERA was encouraging to Theo.

Theo acquired Kim as a starting pitcher, but the thought that he could eventually help out in the bullpen was unavoidable. Kim proceeded to make five starts before the Sox anointed him closer. With that, Theo's ambitious, closer-less bullpen experiment came to an end. Theo was disappointed, but much of the organization was relieved.

Kim went on to post a 3.18 ERA and save 16 games for the Red Sox. Timlin and Embree proved to be Boston's next-best relievers, while Lyon emerged as a decent fourth option. As for the other three spots, there was room for improvement. In addressing the weak spots, Theo showed his inexperience. At the trade deadline, he felt pressure from the media and made an unwise, unnecessary move.

"I was not real happy with the Todd Jones acquisition," said Voros McCracken, then a special consultant to Red Sox Baseball Operations. "It was one of those trades that Theo was pushed into making because of public grip-ing about our bullpen. Particularly in Boston, when pitch-ers go out there and struggle, the crowd gets restless, the papers get restless, and you're forced into making deci-sions you don't want to make."

Jones would go on to appear in 26 games for Boston, pitching to a hideous 5.52 ERA. He made little to no im-pact, resulting in a swing and a miss for Theo. McCracken was right about Jones: it was no surprise to him that the old right-hander was a bust.

It was a learning experience for Theo; the Jones move was the type of ill-advised, media-induced transaction he hoped to avoid in the future. (Yet he would make the same mistake again in 2007, with right-handed reliever Eric Gagné.)

Despite the Jones disaster, the Red Sox's bullpen was decent for the remainder of the regular season—decent enough to keep them in the American League Wild Card race. In the sprint to the finish line, Boston was the first town to tear through the tape. To the surprise of few in the Red Sox organization, Theo led his team to the playoffs in his first official year on the job. The playoff berth would be the first of many major accomplishments for Theo in his new position.

As the regular season came to a close, another of Theo's early triumphs was getting its fair share of attention. This time, Theo was garnering praise for a sneaky, shockingly successful signing he made during his first off-season.

In 2002, the Sox had a revolving door at first base. When the door came to a stop, Brian Daubach, Tony Clark, and Jose Offerman flew off in different directions. Daubach would play for the Sox, but the color of his socks would change. He headed to Chicago to play for the White Sox, while Clark moved on to the Mets. Offerman, falling into obscurity, would not appear in a major league game in 2003.

As a result, the Red Sox's hole at first base was rather deep. Theo decided that the best way to address that hole was an old-fashioned spring training tryout. Enter the five candidates: Jeremy Giambi, Kevin Millar, Dave Nilsson, Earl Snyder, and this other guy, David Ortiz. The quintet of first basemen would also be considered for Boston's designated hitter vacancy.

Out of the pack, Giambi—brother of dangerous Yankees' slugger Jason—was the apple of Theo's eye. Jeremy hit just .259 in 2002, a stat that made him available for (what Theo believed to be) a bargain price. The Red Sox's GM inked Jeremy to a one-year, $2 million contract, a number that paled in comparison to his gaudy .919 OPS. With the Phillies, Jeremy appeared defensively challenged in 21 games at first base, making him a better option as Boston's DH.

Millar was on his way to play professionally in Japan but had a change of heart, signing a two-year deal with Boston worth $5.3 million. Millar had come into his own with the Florida Marlins the previous three years, putting up an OBP of at least .364 each season. He batted over .300 in '01 and '02, as well. Millar was a good defensive first baseman with the versatility to play both corner outfield positions; he and Giambi would definitely be on Theo's 25-man roster, in what capacity, was the only question.

Nilsson, a converted catcher, was an All-Star for the Milwaukee Brewers in 1999. He had been out of the majors for a few seasons, but his solid offensive track record was something for Theo's coaching staff to keep an eye on.

Playing in only 18 games with the Cleveland Indians in '02, Snyder was the long shot of the bunch.

Then there was Ortiz, a large mammal at over 245 pounds. Ortiz had been a highly-regarded prospect in the Minnesota Twins organization for quite some time. Before the Twins and manager Tom Kelly knew it, Ortiz was no longer a "prospect," having played in parts of six seasons with the major league club. The big fella never truly turned the corner, maxing out at 20 homers and 75 RBI in 2002. Injuries were an issue with Ortiz, and the lightly funded Twins opted not to shell out the cash to bring him back in '03.

Theo decided to take a shot on Ortiz, despite his history of physical troubles and a complete lack of defensive value. Ortiz would be suitable on rare occasions at first base, but his limited range and agility took him out of the equation as an everyday option. Theo signed the massive left-handed hitter to a one-year agreement worth $1.25 million.

Twenty homers and 75 RBI for only $1.25 million? Not bad. Ortiz turned out to be a decent gamble.

Yet, behind the scenes, the Red Sox knew he was exactly that: a gamble.

"I was there when people started talking about Ortiz," McCracken said. "It would be a lie to say that we thought he would become the hitter he is today."

But the signing wasn't a total crapshoot for Theo and his talented player evaluation team. He had stuffed his cabinet with versatile baseball minds, and those minds were able to bring Ortiz's strengths to light.

"Everybody was in favor of signing David Ortiz," said senior advisor to Baseball Operations Bill James, in a *60 Minutes* interview. "I liked him because of his numbers, the scouts liked him because of his swing, [and] some people liked him because they knew he was a positive guy in the clubhouse."

Regardless of the behind the scenes discussion, publicly, Theo said all the right things about the man who would later endear himself to everyone (everyone but Yankee fans) as "Big Papi."

"All of our scouts think, and our analysis dictates, that David has a very high ceiling," said Theo. "Due to injuries, he hasn't necessarily reached his ceiling. You're looking at a player who can be an impact middle of the lineup bat. An everyday player. That is his ceiling and we hope he reaches it with us."

Ortiz would go on to reach that ceiling, and mash a

Herculean hole through it, making Theo and his staff look like a panel of rocket scientists.

Ortiz, Millar, and Giambi entered the season in a three-way rotation at first base and designated hitter, and Millar performed well early on, separating himself from his competitors. Unfortunately for the Red Sox, but fortunately for Ortiz and Giambi, Trot Nixon went down with yet another injury, forcing Millar to take over as Boston's primary right fielder. Ortiz would no longer have to look over his shoulder, and his career took off from there.

Ortiz exploded in 2003—not physically, he actually lost a little weight—stunning baseball with 31 homers, 101 RBI, and a sexy .369 on-base percentage; sexy to Theo, of course.

In Byung-Hyun Kim, Theo found a solution for the closer's spot. Millar was the answer at first base. With Ortiz, Theo shored up Boston's designated hitter situation. All of the pieces to a potential championship puzzle were in place as the Red Sox headed into the playoffs.

In the American League Division Series, the Sox squeaked past the Oakland Athletics, winning 4-3 in the decisive game 5. The Athletics' mastermind was Billy Beane, who like Theo, was a studied sabermetrician. The day Theo was named general manager of the Red Sox, Beane was one of his most vocal endorsers.

"There's no time like the present," said Beane. "He's a bright passionate individual. I think the world of Theo. With his passion and intelligence and the people he will surround himself with, he probably can't help but succeed."

The star of *Moneyball* was right on the money; but unfortunately for Beane, Theo's success came at his expense.

Theo and company eventually sold Beane, and he agreed to move his life to Boston. But in a last-second change of heart, Beane decided to remain close to his family in Oakland. There were reportedly no hard feelings between Theo and Beane—and judging by Beane's comments, he seemed to be as fond of Theo as ever—but Theo's first playoff victory had to taste just a little bit sweeter coming against Beane.

Theo also earned the right to think, "Hey, maybe I should have been the first choice from the beginning." And who could argue with him? The Red Sox had reached the American League Championship Series, and had the weapons necessary to win the whole damn thing.

But the big, bad Yankees stood in the way of Theo's World Series dreams. The Red Sox would have to ignore the nightmarish memories of Babe Ruth and Bucky Dent, and fight off "the curse" that had plagued their franchise for decades. With an experienced core in Roger Clemens, Derek Jeter, Andy Pettitte, Jorge Posada, Bernie Williams, and Mariano Rivera, the Yankees were battle-tested. Any attack the Sox were planning, these guys had seen it. Theo's boys most certainly had their hands full.

It would prove to be a hotly contested, back-and-forth series. The Sox jumped out to a 1-0 series lead at Yankee

Stadium, and the Bombers answered back with a 6-2 victory in game 2. Like the Sox, the Yankees won their first road game of the series, holding on at Fenway by the score of 4-3. Boston tied the series, squeaking out a 3-2 win in game 4, and New York fired back, taking game 5.

Following the back-and-forth progression of the series was like watching Rocky Balboa and Ivan Drago go haymaker-for-haymaker in *Rocky IV*.

Facing elimination in game 6, Theo's club answered the call. Garciaparra smacked four hits, and "Theo guys" Ortiz and Bill Mueller (his third baseman) also produced on the big stage. Mueller stroked three hits and scored a run, and Ortiz provided two hits and three critical RBI en route to a 9-6 victory over the combination of Andy Pettitte, Jose Contreras, Felix Heredia, Jeff Nelson, and Gabe White. It was a rough night for the Yankee pitching staff, Heredia had the only exceptional performance of the evening—two-thirds of an inning's worth the scoreless work. Nice game.

So it was time for Theo, the rest of Boston's front office, and all of Red Sox Nation to sweat it out during game 7. The decisive game would pit two potential Hall of Famers, Roger Clemens of the Yankees and Pedro Martinez of the Sox, against one another. Major League Baseball couldn't have scripted it any better.

Clemens, battling injuries and a confident Boston lineup, would pitch only three innings, allowing four runs (three earned) on six hits. With Pedro on the hill and cruising through the first three innings, it looked as if Theo was well on the way to the first American League Championship of his general managerial career. Pedro couldn't possibly blow a four-run lead, could he?

Well, it was Yankees-Red Sox... anything could happen.

Pedro took that 4-0 lead into the fifth inning, only to have his shutout erased by a Jason Giambi home run to lead off the inning. But Pedro wasn't rattled by the homer; he worked confidently into the eighth inning with a 5-2 lead. Two, three, and four—Nick Johnson, Derek Jeter, and Bernie Williams—were due up in the vaunted Yankee lineup, but Grady Little was sticking with his man. It was Pedro's game to lose, even more so than anyone had realized at the time.

The Evil Empire had no intention of going quietly. Pedro would be put to the test—as would Little—and Theo was watching closely. If the Sox's skipper could go back in time, he'd probably be a bit wearier of Theo's gaze over his shoulder.

Johnson popped up to begin the inning, and Pedro, Theo, and the rest of the Sox's organization were five outs away from the World Series. The way the remainder of the inning played out, the five outs may well have been fifty. The Yankees weren't going to let Pedro shut the door on them. Forget about the ninth inning, Boston had to figure out a way to stop the bleeding in the eighth.

Jeter and Williams, the seasoned playoff veterans, put together back-to-back hits off Pedro. Jeter doubled and

Bernie knocked him in with a single to center. Hideki Matsui followed with a double of his own, and the Yankees had the tying runs in scoring position with one out, and switch-hitting catcher Jorge Posada at the plate.

Little asked for time, and strolled out to the mound. Theo anxiously awaited his manager's decision.

Boston had a pair of relievers warming in the bullpen: right-hander Mike Timlin and lefty Alan Embree. Making the move for Embree would force Posada over to the right side of the plate, his weaker side. Embree was one of the Sox's better relievers, but was far from spectacular in '03. He maintained his plus fastball, but hitters seemed to have adjusted to it. Was switching Posada over to the other side worth bringing in an inferior pitcher? That's what Little had to weigh in his mind. Pedro was gassed, but even a tired Pedro had to be considered better than a fresh Embree.

Decisions, decisions. Little's move would go down as one of the most debated in the history of baseball.

After an animated conference on the mound in which he appeared to be feeling Pedro out, getting a sense of his pitcher's confidence and stamina, Little opted to stay with his ace. Embree would continue warming alongside Timlin, and Pedro would face Posada on his stronger side.

Unfortunately for Little, Pedro failed to reward him for his faith. Posada dropped in a bloop double, scoring both Williams and Matsui and tying the game at five. With the score tied, the Sox weren't completely finished, but Little was… he just didn't know it yet.

Embree and Timlin would battle to record the final two outs of the inning, and the ballgame remained tied until the bottom of the 11th inning. Boston's bullpen was wearing thin, so Little turned to Tim Wakefield, the veteran knuckleballer who had worked as both a starter and reliever in his career.

Up to the plate marched the No. 8 batter, corner infielder Aaron Boone, and as they say… the rest is history.

Boone emphatically stamped his name beside Babe Ruth and Bucky Dent, launching a no-doubter of a home run into the left-field seats at Yankee Stadium.

Wakefield, expressionless, lumbered slowly off the mound as Boone danced around the bases and the Yankee faithful went bonkers. Theo had suffered his first truly stomach-twisting, heart-breaking, tear-inducing loss as the Boston Red Sox's general manager. Given the club's history, it seemed that similarly painful losses were on the horizon—unless Theo did something about it.

He started by letting Little go. On October 28, 2003, Theo and the rest of Boston's front office made it clear that they would not pick up Little's contractual option for the 2004 season. Reporters bombarded Theo at the press conference, repeatedly asking if Little had been fired because of his decision to stick with Pedro in the eighth inning of game 7.

"All I can tell you is the truth, which is quite simply that the decision was made on a body of work after careful contemplation of the big picture," Theo said. "It did not depend on any one decision in any one postseason game."

Some people naturally took Theo for a liar. Little helped the Red Sox amass a 95-67 record and led them to the playoffs; both were improvements over the previous year. Boston was one game away from the World Series, somewhere they hadn't been since 1986. The Sox were ousted by the Yankees who had been to the World Series in five of the previous seven seasons—winning it thrice—so it wasn't as if the Sox lost to an unqualified or undeserving opponent. Little's undoing had to be the decision to leave Pedro out there. If Boston had pulled out the victory and went on to the Big Dance, would he still have been fired?

Of course not. Sure, Little was a holdover from the Dan Duquette regime, but if he led the Red Sox to the World Series he wasn't going anywhere. In the end, even if Boston lost to the Florida Marlins (as the Yankees eventually did), letting Little walk would have resulted in too much heat for Theo to take.

One bad decision and Theo let his manager go? Was it even a "bad" decision? It may have been the "wrong" choice, but Embree could have easily given up the big hit to Posada. Maybe it was a lose-lose for Little, maybe he was doomed either way. There's no way of knowing, but at the time, everyone seemed to assume that Pedro's replacement would have gotten the job done—a totally unfair assumption. Well-respected *Boston Globe* columnist, Bob Ryan, wrote, "Grady Little's own heart overruled his head."

Would he have written that if Posada's little blooper had been caught? Pedro made a quality pitch to Posada, and the Yankees' catcher failed to put good wood on it. If Embree had entered in that spot and surrendered a rocket to blow the game, many would have been saying, "Why did Little yank his ace in favor of a journeyman middle reliever?"

The point being, staying with his superstar wasn't a horrible decision. At least seven times out of ten, Pedro retires Posada under those circumstances. Was one decision enough to make Theo look in a different managerial direction?

To this day, some would say "yes." It was a sticky situation, and Theo moved on from it by bringing in a new manager—the first he could call his own. In arguably the most successful signing of his young career, Theo inked Terry Francona, formerly the bench coach of the Oakland Athletics, to a three-year deal with a team option for a fourth.

"When we started this process about five or six weeks ago, we knew we were looking for somebody who could excel both in the clubhouse and in the dugout," Theo said. "Somebody who had an optimum commitment to preparation; somebody who has the integrity and interpersonal skills to forge meaningful relationships; someone who would be a dynamic partner for the front office as we continue to build the organization—we feel that we found all those things and more in Terry Francona."

Francona was an experienced baseball man, an ex-manager of the Philadelphia Phillies, but he had two very specific things working for him in Boston: he familiarized himself with sabermetrics in his time working for GM Billy Beane in Oakland, and he dealt with eccentric pitcher Curt Schilling—Theo's most recent, big-name acquisition—during his tenure in Philadelphia. Francona was qualified for the job to begin with, but those additional tidbits of information made him all the more impressive to Theo.

It was a completely and utterly disappointing end to the 2003 season for Theo and the rest of Red Sox Nation, but things were looking up during the '03-04 off-season. In '04, it couldn't get much worse than a walk-off loss in game 7 of the ALCS to the repulsive Yankees—could it?

Theo had that to bank on, and the additions of Schilling and Francona added to an increasing sense of optimism. Theo's third and final impact pick-up was crafty closer Keith Foulke—last a member of the Athletics (another connection to Beane)—who would bring more stability to the back of Boston's bullpen than Byung-Hyun Kim had in '03. Kim would stick around temporarily, but in a lesser capacity.

In spite of the Schilling, Francona, and Foulke acquisitions, it was the move that Theo failed to make that received the most off-season attention.

The Red Sox were undoubtedly one of the most talented teams in the majors in 2003, but like any good general manager, Theo knew there was room for improvement. Roster management requires activity, not stagnation, and opportunities to upgrade must be capitalized upon. With that in mind, the potential upgrade was enormous in this situation. This time, Theo and Lucchino weren't just chasing an All-Star…

They were chasing Alex Rodriguez, the best ballplayer in the universe.

"A-Rod," the 6-foot-3 all-world shortstop of the Texas Rangers, was coming off a season where he played in 161 games, hitting 47 homers and driving in 118 runs while sporting a .396 on-base percentage. Those numbers, combined with his heady base running and excellent defense, earned him the first Most Valuable Player Award of his sensational eight-year career.

So the Rangers had the reigning American League MVP, a durable player who could do no wrong on a baseball diamond. Why the hell did they want to trade him?

For starters, the Rangers finished dead last in the AL Western Division in 2003. That fact made A-Rod's victory in the MVP race all the more impressive. The voters rarely ever give the award to a player on a losing team, let alone a last-place team. Yet from the Rangers' perspective, namely that of owner Tom Hicks and general manager John Hart, Rodriguez was expendable because he wasn't helping their club win.

And then there was another little issue, A-Rod's contract. The show-stopping shortstop was heading into the fourth year of a record-breaking 10-year contract worth $252 million.

Hart could make Hicks extremely happy by dumping the remaining seven years of Rodriguez's deal on another team, and picking up a quality player in return. No matter who came back in Texas' direction, they *had* to be making less than A-Rod. A trade made sense for the Rangers, they didn't appear to be going anywhere with the 252-Million Dollar Man anyway.

But clearly, given the dollars and cents of A-Rod's contract, only a handful of other teams could afford him. Fortunately for Theo, the Red Sox were one of them.

Theo had one big chip to offer: Manny Ramirez. Without question, Ramirez was one of the premier hitters in the bigs—particularly in the clutch—but he didn't compare to Rodriguez as an all-around player. In addition, Ramirez was a loose cannon. A fun guy, a guy his teammates could laugh and joke around with, but a player who would sometimes jog out of the box on a possible double-play ball, dive for a fly ball he couldn't possibly get to, or walk all the way to first admiring one of his home runs. Sometimes he'd watch one go, but it would stay in the yard, costing him an extra base. There was no denying Manny's talent, but he was often difficult for managers, coaches, and executives to deal with.

He may have been tough to handle, but Manny was still an exceptional hitter making less money than A-Rod. The Rangers had finished last in their division four consecutive seasons, so they had little to lose. What they could gain, was the monetary difference between the two stars' contracts. Manny's deal, like A-Rod's, began with the 2001 season, but it was an eight-year agreement worth $160 million. A massive contract, yes, but it was not nearly as eye-popping as A-Rod's.

Hart and Hicks would take the bait, but there was so much money involved that the Rangers and Red Sox requested permission to negotiate finances before the trade was made official. Commissioner Bud Selig agreed to let them talk money, but the two sides' efforts went for naught when the Players Association took a hatchet to the deal. Theo, Henry, and Lucchino were looking to restructure Rodriguez's contract, but understandably, the Players Association wouldn't allow their largest contract to shrink.

Theo wasn't able to bring A-Rod to Beantown. Unfortunately, his troubles only began there.

The A-Rod negotiations were overly public; quite simply, everyone knew too much. When it looked as if the Rodriguez-for-Ramirez deal was inevitable, word got out that Theo would follow up with another blockbuster move. He would ship his franchise shortstop, Nomar Garciaparra—the face of the Red Sox—to the Chicago White Sox for potent outfielder Magglio Ordonez. A-Rod would take over for Nomar, and Ordonez would replace Manny.

When word reached Nomar, he was taken aback. Stunned, insulted, and just plain hurt, Nomar put on his puss face. He kept it that way for the remainder of his stay in Boston. Theo was left with a disgruntled shortstop at the very end of his prime.

To make matters worse, another team was able to pull off a trade for A-Rod. That team was, of course, the dream-crushing New York Yankees. The Aaron Boone homer had to be rock bottom, but this was one hell of an encore. Red Sox Nation took another heavy blow, but as always, it remained firmly on its feet. Before long, Boston's faithful would be rewarded for their dedication and resiliency.

The reward came quicker than any of them could have expected.

Even without A-Rod, Theo's club had it all heading into Boston's magical 2004 season—strong starters, good relievers, a prolific offense, solid defense, and a hungry, aggressive manager. Interestingly enough, "Duquette guys" still accounted for a significant portion of the roster, a credit to the talented-but-volatile former GM. But in just one full season (and two off-seasons) Theo had plugged many of the holes that kept Duquette's 2002 team out of the postseason. From '02 to '03, under Theo, the Sox went from playoff contender to World Series contender. Looking ahead to '04, they had to be considered one of the favorites to win it all. The missing pieces were Millar, Mueller, Ortiz, Schilling, Foulke, and Francona—all products of the Epstein regime.

With two seasons as general manager under his belt

(one official, one not), Theo was completely settled into his role.

"Theo did an excellent job of keeping us focused on baseball," said Voros McCracken, a former Epstein cabinet member. "In terms of analyzing baseball, he was willing to let us talk about various topics, but as soon as we got a little too far off topic, he would get us back on task—immediately."

McCracken said Theo had a mindset exuding "controlled thoughtfulness." He also complimented Theo's ability to gather his thoughts quickly, and organize them at a similar rate.

And yet, despite Theo's focus and the strength of his roster, the Sox stumbled out of the gate in the new season. To add injury to insult in the Garciaparra saga, Nomar missed the opening nine weeks of the season with Achilles tendonitis. Trot Nixon was also battling an injury, and starting pitchers Derek Lowe and Tim Wakefield struggled in the early going. Lastly, in the bullpen, Foulke got roughed up in his first week with the Sox, and Kim pitched poorly enough to make himself unusable in the eyes of Terry Francona.

However, Pedro and Schilling were throwing well, and Ortiz, Manny, and Johnny Damon were tearing the cover off the ball. Theo still had plenty of faith in his players, and he hoped that Nomar's return would provide the physical and emotional boost needed for his club to perform up to the level of its enormous payroll.

In fact, Nomar's return would do just the opposite: put the Sox in an even greater funk. Nomar managed to produce in drips and drabs, but the Achilles injury turned him into one the worst defensive shortstops in baseball and his attitude for the game was at an all-time low. Reports were that he would often complain to his teammates about Red Sox's management, and he looked as if he didn't care anymore. Didn't care about his performance, didn't care about winning, and didn't care about Boston.

Nomar Garciaparra, the Red Sox's headliner from 1997 to 2003, was now a cancer in Theo Epstein's ball club. It was time for him to go.

Theo had a couple of other shortstops on his roster, Calvin "Pokey" Reese and Ricky Gutierrez, but neither were long-term solutions. Reese rightfully had a reputation as one of the premier defensive middle infielders in the league, but he brought little to nothing offensively. His history of injuries made it even more difficult for Theo to see him as an everyday option.

Gutierrez was a better hitter than Reese, but that's not saying much. With no range and a weakening arm, Gutierrez was a train wreck defensively, and his 12-year major league career was on its last legs. He was a third-stringer/25th man on a roster, at best.

If Nomar was going to be traded, Theo had to exchange him for another shortstop. The Sox lacked a legitimate internal option, so they had to look elsewhere. When the tricky transaction wheel came to a stop, Theo landed on Orlando Cabrera, the shortstop of the Montreal Expos.

Cabrera, a right-handed hitter under six feet tall, was having a down season offensively—.246, four homers, 31 RBI—but had displayed considerable pop in recent years. He hit .297 with 17 homers and 80 RBI in 2003, and posted 14 homers with 96 RBI in 2001. Such numbers were chump change to Garciaparra, who was clearly the superior hitter of the two, but Cabrera held the edge in both fielding and base running. The little fella stole at least 24 bases in each of the prior two seasons, while Nomar maxed out at 19. With the injuries, he wouldn't get anywhere near that total in '04.

On July 31, 2004, Theo traded Nomar to the Chicago Cubs in a four-way deal that landed him Cabrera and Minnesota Twins' first baseman Doug Mientkiewicz.

In Boston, an era had officially come to an end.

"It was with mixed emotions that we let Nomar go," said Theo. "He's been one of the greatest Red Sox of all time."

Maybe so, but Nomar's attitude, injuries, and defense had all become major detriments to the Sox. Cabrera was the National League Gold Glove winner in 2001, and Mientkiewicz boasted a Gold Glove of his own. Once again, Theo accurately identified his club's weaknesses.

"I thought there was a flaw on the club that we couldn't allow to become a fatal flaw, that the defense on this team is not championship caliber," Theo said. "In my mind we were not going to win a World Series with our defense the way it was."

With Nomar out of the picture, the Red Sox took off. In 45 less games with Boston, Cabrera matched his Expos' RBI total of 31. He hit two more homers, with six, and his batting average jumped 48 points to .294. Mientkiewicz played flawless defense in place of Kevin Millar, who was again forced into the outfield in Nixon's absence.

Theo's stars continued to do their job, and his role players finally got up to speed. Boston went on to finish the regular season with a 98-64 record, landing Terry Francona in the playoffs in his first year as manager. As far as postseason appearances went, Theo was batting a thousand (two-for-two).

Out of the American League Wild Card spot, the Red Sox spanked the Anaheim Angels in the Division Series, scoring 25 runs in just three games. In their sweep of the best-of-five, eight was the *least* amount of runs the Sox scored in a game. Over the course of the three victories, Manny hit .385, Damon .467, and Ortiz .545. To the Big Three, Angels' pitchers weren't firing baseballs to the plate... they were floating beach balls. Theo's thunderous triumvirate could do no wrong; he could only hope that their rousing success would continue into the ALCS.

In yet another example of poetic justice in baseball, the Red Sox would have a chance to redeem themselves against the Yankees in the ALCS. Considering the previous year's thrilling seven-game series, this was the match-up nearly everyone wanted to see—the greatest rivalry in sports at its highest possible level. Of course, the Yankees and Red Sox could never meet in the World Series, so this was it. It couldn't get any bigger… or better.

What ensued was the most incredible team comeback in the history of athletics.

Before Theo could blink, his team was in an 0-2 series hole. The Yankees weren't interested in playing seven games this time around; they intended to bury the Red Sox and stomp over their graves on the way to the World Series.

Schilling, battling a severe ankle injury (a retinaculum tear) got destroyed in game 1, allowing six earned runs in just three innings. Alex Rodriguez, Gary Sheffield, Bernie Williams, and Hideki Matsui all had at least two hits for New York in its 10-7 victory.

Game 2 was a bit more competitive, with the Yankees squeaking it out by the final score of 3-1. The Sox were in it, but Theo's normally productive lineup mustered up only five hits against Yankee pitching. Jon Lieber, Tom Gordon, and Mariano Rivera combined on the win for the Yanks.

The series moved to Fenway Park for game 3, an absolute must-win for the Sox; or at least, that's what history dictated. In Major League Baseball's 101-year lifespan, no team had ever come back from a 3-0 deficit to win a postseason series. In fact, no team had ever forced a game 6 after falling behind 3-0.

The Red Sox had to win game 3, and they didn't. Theo's stomach turned inside out as he watched the Yankees pound his boys, banging out 22 hits en route to 19 runs and an 11-run victory. The Yankees hit four home runs in the game—two by Matsui—and Francona had to use six pitchers in the process. The Sox were bruised, battered, and beaten heading into game 4, and the Yankees once again seemed to embrace the role of Grim Reaper.

Theo was distraught. According to *Reversing the Curse*, Theo's friends—front office members Jed Hoyer, Peter Woodfork, and Jonathan Gilula—were worried about what he might do following the embarrassing blowout in game 3. The trio insisted that Theo hang out at their apartment, where he would eventually suck down five vodka tonics and watch the replay of the "Aaron Boone game" from the previous year. It certainly seemed like a battle with post-devastating-loss depression, and in the midst of it, Theo openly acknowledged that his club needed a miracle to win the series.

As it turned out, they needed more than just one miracle to pull off the earth-shattering comeback. Or maybe they weren't miracles at all; maybe the Red Sox earned every single bit of their momentous accomplishment. Either way, the road to redemption began in game 4.

The Yankees jumped out to a 2-0 lead, and the Red

Sox stormed back with three runs off Orlando "El Duque" Hernandez in the fifth. The Yanks regained the lead with two off Derek Lowe in the sixth, and carried their one-run advantage into the ninth inning, the inning owned by Mariano Rivera. Rivera is arguably the best closer in the history of the game, but the Red Sox had given him trouble earlier in '04. Theo could only hope that his club's relative success against Rivera would continue; otherwise, it would be two consecutive ALCS losses to the hated Yankees. This one, a sweep, would be nearly impossible to swallow.

Fittingly enough, Millar walked to lead off the inning. It was a fitting start to the drama because sabermetricians like Theo absolutely love walks, and this one came off a pitcher with impeccable control. Rivera rarely ever gave away a free base, a credit to Millar's eye and Theo's baseball philosophy. Leadoff runners are often the key to comebacks, and the Red Sox had theirs.

There was only one problem: Millar would be lucky to beat a fatigued sumo wrestler in a race.

All right, he wasn't that slow, but he was a long shot to score from first on a double. Terry Francona looked to his bench for a pinch runner. Off the pine jogged Dave Roberts, a reserve outfielder with game-changing speed. Roberts had been a starter with the Los Angeles Dodgers earlier in the season, but in an effort to strengthen his bench and increase its versatility, Theo acquired Roberts around the same time as Cabrera and Mientkiewicz.

Roberts hadn't seen much playing time with the Sox; nonetheless, the organization was counting on him in the biggest spot of the year.

It quickly became clear that Roberts wasn't in there to score from first on a double... he was planning to score from second on a single. Rivera delivered and Roberts took off for second, blistering down the baseline. Yankees' catcher Jorge Posada came up with a strong throw, but on a close play, Roberts slid in safely with a stolen base. The Red Sox were in business. Theo saw hope.

Almost instantaneously, Bill Mueller followed with a single up the middle. Roberts blazed around third to score, and the Sox had tied the game before Rivera could record an out. The Yankees' closer eventually escaped after the Mueller RBI, pushing the game into extra innings.

In the bottom of the twelfth, Manny started the inning with a single off veteran right-hander Paul Quantrill. Manny was never one to bust it around the bases. He always preferred to jog, and that's exactly what he got to do in the twelfth. The very next batter, David Ortiz—the man so many teams opted to pass on, the man Theo originally signed for just $1.25 million—sent one soaring over the right field fence and into the fond memories of Red Sox fans everywhere.

There would be no sweep. Theo could breathe a sigh of relief, but one win wasn't enough. There are no consolation prizes in Major League Baseball; Theo wanted his guys to come back and win the series. Anything less would have been a disappointment.

Having learned about the superstitious nature of the game in recent years, Theo dismissed his logic and sophisticated intuition, and went back to the home of his front office buddies. He decided that the apartment where he drank himself to sleep might have been his four-leaf clover. Theo couldn't know for sure, but he wasn't about to mess with karma.

"Big Papi" struck again in game 5, squeezing out a game winning single off Esteban Loaiza in the bottom of the 14th. For the Yankees, Papi's soft hit had to be eerily reminiscent of Luis Gonzalez's World Series-winning blooper in 2001. Were the baseball gods trying to warn the Bronx Bombers?

They may have been. The Yankees should have listened.

Theo, meanwhile, listened to the little leprechaun in his ear. Before the third and final game at Fenway Park, he hung out with Hoyer, Woodfork, and Gilula—again. Theo would sleep at their apartment, waking up a little more confident about the outcome of the next game.

Carried by Curt Schilling's awe-inspiring, bloody sock performance in game 6, Theo's men forced a game 7 at Yankee Stadium, becoming the first team to fight back from a 3-0 deficit to tie the series. Schilling gritted his way through seven gutsy innings, allowing just one run on four hits. Foulke picked up the save, his first of the series.

Iron Man Shilling

Heading into game 7, Red Sox Nation was rejuvenated. It would be painful for the Sox to battle back feverishly and lose, but this time around, the positive thoughts seemed to outweigh the negatives. Something about the progression of the series suggested that Babe Ruth's ghost was slowly but surely fading away. On Boston's side, no one was talking about the curse, or Bucky Dent; everyone seemed to be focused on the 2004 Red Sox, and nothing else.

Theo wouldn't be able to stay over his friends' apartment before game 7 in New York, but all of a sudden, he wasn't too concerned. It was simple, Theo thought that his players could finish the job, and so did they. The Yankees had to be mentally exhausted, and they had to be questioning if they had the heart to match the "bunch of idiots" (Damon's nickname for the Sox) in the opposing dugout.

As it turned out, they didn't.

The Red Sox steamrolled the Yankees in the decisive game 7, scoring 10 runs on 13 hits and limiting New York to just three runs on five hits. It was total domination, highlighted by Damon's upper-deck grand slam off Javier Vazquez in the top of the second, and six innings of one-hit ball from starting pitcher Derek Lowe. Lowe could never seem to figure it out during the regular season, and yet he put together his best performance of the year in its highest-pressure game—just another example of the incredible character assembled on Theo Epstein's 2004 Boston Red Sock roster.

"That's for the '03 team, just like it's for the '78 and the '49 team," Theo said after his team's astonishing comeback. "I hope Ted Williams is having a cocktail upstairs."

Clearly, Theo was elated. A year earlier, when Aaron Boone unleashed the bomb that obliterated Boston's World Series hopes, Red Sox Nation wondered if it could get any worse. With New York's victory in the race for A-Rod, it almost did. When the Yankees took the commanding 3-0 lead in the ALCS, there was the stomach-sinking sense of, "Ugh, here we go again."

And yet, in spite of the Red Sox's history of painful

failures, it was the Yankees who would suffer the most heart-crushing defeat of all. There's no getting around it—in the most storied rivalry in professional sports, at its highest possible level, there is nothing worse than blowing a 3-0 series lead. New York lost the final two games on the hallowed grounds of Yankee Stadium, no less.

"I'm embarrassed," said Alex Rodriguez. "Obviously that hurts—watching them on our field celebrating."

It was embarrassing, and Theo Epstein was the mastermind behind the worst choke-job in the history of the Yankees' mythical franchise. It was Theo's boys who brought their archrivals to an all-time low.

From there, it was a piece of cake. If the Red Sox could come back from 3-0 to win against the Yanks, they had to be able to handle the St. Louis Cardinals in a best-of-seven, right?

Well, Theo's actions suggested that he wasn't so sure.

"I'm sitting next to Theo at the '04 Series in St. Louis, and he's nervous," said Bill Lajoie, then the 70-year-old assistant to the general manager. "We had just won seven in a row, and he's sitting there, folding his arms and fidgeting. I looked over at him and said, 'Hey, take it easy, just sit and watch the game. The players will take care of it. There's nothing we can do now but watch and enjoy.'"

Theo promptly unfolded his arms, put his hands on his knees, and did his best to watch the game calmly. As it turned out, he had nothing to worry about.

Theo's gang finished the job against the Cardinals,

sweeping Tony LaRussa's Redbirds into World Series obscurity. The Red Sox were too confident, too determined... hell, they were just too damn good.

When Mientkiewicz caught the final out, Theo could finally slide off the edge of his seat. With the tension completely relieved, it was time for Theo to let go. It was time to take it all in, if that was even possible. And of course, it was time to party.

Theo and his players were high off life, partying deep into the evening and on into the next day. There were no words to describe it; few have articulated what World Series glory is like.

Thirty years old, and a World Series champion.

Thirty years old, and the savior of a franchise infamous for 86 years of catastrophe and failure.

Thirty years old, and they couldn't call him "The Wonder Boy" anymore...

He was "The Man."

Boston's Prodigal Son Steps Down

Theo may have been "The Man" in Boston after the Red Sox's historic 2004 season, but things can change quickly in Beantown. There would be no repeat in 2005—his club followed up with a disappointing campaign in which they were swept out of the first round of the playoffs by the Chicago White Sox, the eventual World Series victors. BoSox fans didn't seem to care; they had their revenge against the Yankees and their long-awaited championship, and anything else was gravy. There were no changes in the way Theo was received by the fans—they still loved him; the changes were occurring behind the scenes, in the Red Sox's front office. The spotlight that followed Theo from the day he was named the youngest GM in Major League Baseball history, flickered, and began to fade. Soon, Theo would slip away, and his fans would be left behind in the dark.

On October 31, 2005, Theo Epstein abruptly resigned from his position as general manager of the Boston Red Sox.

Red Sox Nation was shocked, stunned, and dismayed. The man who shaped the team that ended 86 years of suffering, the one who the ladies adored and the men thanked for turning things around, was gone—just like that. Very few people, inside of baseball or out, saw it coming. What looked like a match made in heaven, a magical marriage between man and franchise, was actually a ticking time bomb ready to explode. When the timer went off, the minds of many were blown.

Scratching their heads, everyone could only wonder, "What the hell happened?"

For starters, Theo issued a statement addressed to the media, the Red Sox, and his fans:

> First, I want to thank John Henry, Tom Werner, and Larry Lucchino for the opportunity to serve as general manager for the last three seasons. Their support and friendship mean a lot to me, and I wish them all well. I also owe a debt of gratitude to the players, Terry Francona, the coaching staff, the front office, the baseball operations staff, and the fans for making my Red Sox experience so meaningful.
>
> Growing up in the shadow of Fenway Park, I never dreamed of having the chance to work for my hometown team during such an historic period.

My decision not to return as general manager of the Red Sox is an extremely difficult one. I will always cherish the relationships I developed here and am proud to have worked side-by-side with so many great people, in and out of uniform, as together we brought a world championship to Boston.

In my time as general manager, I gave my entire heart and soul to the organization. During the process leading up to today's decision, I came to the conclusion that I can no longer do so. In the end, my choice is the right one not only for me but for the Red Sox.

My affection for the Red Sox did not begin four years ago when I started working here, and it does not end today. I will remain on the job for several days as we finalize preparation for next week's general managers meetings. Thereafter, I will make myself available to the organization to ensure a smooth and stable transition.

My passion for and dedication to the game of baseball remain strong. Although I have no immediate plans, I will embrace this change in my life and look forward with excitement to the future.

With that statement came very little explanation. The only thing that Sox fans could take from the message was that Theo could no longer give his "heart and soul to the organization," but even that said virtually nothing.

What was missing was the "why." Why couldn't Theo devote his heart and soul?

Those who read Theo's statement closely found contradictions in his speech. He said, "My affection for the Red Sox did not begin four years ago… and it does not end today," and "my passion for and dedication to the game of baseball remain strong." Put the two together: "I love the Red Sox, and want to continue working in baseball."

That didn't seem to match with the "can't devote himself to the Red Sox" line. The entire statement stank like a steaming pile of bullshit. Something fishy had happened, and since Theo refused to clarify his decision, the public was left to speculate and discuss. The vast majority of that discussion focused on two things: (1) The contract offer he had received from the Red Sox and (2) his relationship with president and CEO Larry Lucchino.

"While the initial differences in Epstein's negotiations centered on money," the *Boston Globe*'s Chris Snow wrote, "those issues were bridged, to the point that multiple major league sources said over the weekend that Epstein and the club had come to an agreement on an extension.

"However, issues of respect and control between Epstein and CEO/president Larry Lucchino could not be overcome," Snow continued, "ultimately leading Epstein,

31, to reject the club's three-year, $4.5 million offer and give up what might well have been the only job he ever wanted."

Almost across the board, outside sources echoed Snow's notion about the situation with Lucchino; but we'll get to that in a little while. Let's take another look at the contract offer—it may have had more to do with the problems between Theo and Lucchino than the media and public tended to believe.

A three-year, $4.5 million contract would bring Theo $1.5 million annually. There was something very significant about those numbers, and that offer. Three years earlier, during the off-season prior to Theo's first season as general manager, Lucchino's first choice for the vacancy was Oakland's Billy Beane. He offered Beane a record-breaking five-year deal worth $12.5 million, an average of $2.5 million per season. Three years later, Beane was still without a World Series title, but Theo, on the other hand, had a sparkling ring on his finger.

Why would Lucchino offer Theo $1 million less than Beane, annually? Sure Beane had more experience as a GM, and Oakland's financial situation was more difficult to deal with than Boston's, but the fact remained that Beane's boys had never even been to the World Series. Theo put together a team that got there, and won—he wasn't worth the same $2.5 million per season that Lucchino offered Beane three years earlier?

Apparently not. The offer didn't make sense, because

the Red Sox's faithful embraced Theo, and it wasn't as if John Henry lacked the funding to reward him. Theo's youth also worked in his favor because he had already been to the top, and had plenty of time to continue improving and refining his general managerial tactics. He was like a young player in his prime: worth the long-term commitment, and worth a little extra money.

Here's the kicker: $4.5 million over three years is what Theo negotiated his way up to. That's the contract he *asked* for, which means Lucchino was really low-balling him before that. Theo rejected a deal that would have paid him $1.2 million per season.

Why the crappy contract offers? Why would Lucchino insult Theo, the kid he was introduced to in Baltimore, the young man that impressed him in San Diego, the professional he worked side-by-side with in Boston?

What it looked like was a power play on Lucchino's part. He knew he could give Theo $2.5 million a year and no one in Boston would bat an eye, and yet he started negotiations around $1 million per season, maybe even less.

However, from Lucchino's point of view, there was an X-factor: Theo's 2004 World Series bonus. The extent of that bonus has never been revealed, but Bill Lajoie, former Detroit Tigers general manager, said he received about twenty percent of his salary after constructing a World Series champion in 1984. His guess was that Theo received a similar percentage, or perhaps more, considering the change in times. Point being, Theo was doing very well financially, and Lucchino knew it. If he could use that fact to save Henry and Werner a little money in the negotiations, then he would.

Regardless, Lucchino's initial contract offer was a cheap shot. Interestingly enough, it wasn't the first time he had taken one at Theo.

The silent battle between Theo and Lucchino—in which Lucchino was the aggressor—began in December of 2003, when the Red Sox hoped to trade for Alex Rodriguez. Theo worked hard to come to an agreement with Texas Rangers' GM John Hart, and it finally looked like they had one involving Manny Ramirez. When the trade was proposed to the Players Association, it didn't go over too well. The union wanted massive restructuring, and it looked as if Theo and Lucchino would have to go back to the drawing board.

Lucchino had no intention of doing so quietly. He made the following public statement:

> Theo Epstein and his staff worked diligently and tirelessly and reached an agreement with Alex Rodriguez. Theo had the full support of John, Tom, and me along the way. The Red Sox and Rangers had agreed to the players to be involved in this transaction and were working toward an agreement on financial considerations to be included. A lot of time and effort has been invested on all sides to reach this critical point, but the Players

Association rejected the agreement Alex took to them and, instead, proposed radical changes.

It is a sad day when the Players Association thwarts the will of its members. The Players Association asserts that it supports individual negotiations, freedom of choice, and player mobility. However, in this high-profile instance, their action contradicts this and is contrary to the desires of the player.

Lucchino attacked the Players Association while appearing to speak on Theo's behalf. By opening with "Theo Epstein and his staff," Lucchino made his statement from Theo's perspective, throwing his young GM under the bus and opening him up to criticism that should have been aimed entirely at his hot-headed superior. Not only did Lucchino upset the Players Union, but Rangers' owner Tom Hicks was also steamed about the comments. He was upset by Lucchino's lack of professionalism, and soured on the idea of negotiating with a businessman who would make such ill-advised public comments.

It was Lucchino who put the final dagger in the A-Rod to Boston deal, not the Players Association. In the process he tarnished his own reputation, and brought Theo down with him. It was a slimy move on Lucchino's part, but Theo chose to be the bigger man, and ignored it for the time being.

But the memory of the A-Rod debacle lingered in Theo's mind during the 2005 contract negotiations.

Lucchino, too, was upset. His displeasure stemmed from the articles that ESPN's Peter Gammons was writing about Boston's front office. Gammons, a Hall of Fame baseball insider, continued to cover the Red Sox's situation, seemingly always tilting his columns in favor of Theo. If Lucchino left Theo out to dry with the public statement about the Players Association, then it seemed that Theo had returned the favor with the Gammons stories. Theo and Gammons were known to be friends; the former was an avid participant in the latter's charity events.

On both ends, emotions boiled. With the modest contract offers, it seemed that Lucchino was trying to remind Theo of their history: Theo was an intern in Baltimore—Lucchino was president and CEO; Theo was director of Baseball Operations in San Diego—Lucchino was president and CEO. Wherever they went, Lucchino was Theo's clear superior. Yet in Boston Theo had become the town's prodigal son, and in doing so, he received much of the credit that Lucchino was rumored to desire.

"One guy loves going on radio and TV shows, the other guy hated it. One guy loves the power rush of running a team; the other guy just liked making baseball moves. One guy loved getting credit, the other guy didn't care. But both guys wanted the car keys," wrote ESPN columnist Bill Simmons shortly after Theo's departure.

And he was right. Yet in spite of that troubling dynamic, Theo was within a hair of signing that $4.5 million contract and returning to the Sox. What stopped him was another public shot taken by Lucchino. This time he didn't say a word, but his overbearing presence was felt in a *Boston Globe* column written by Dan Shaughnessy, the same man that Theo devoted hours to for *Reversing the Curse*. The column, entitled "Let's iron out some of this dirty laundry," represented a double stab in Theo's back.

Shaughnessy wrote:

> The Theo-Larry story is as old as the Bible. Mentor meets protege. Mentor teaches young person all he knows. Eventually, the prodigy is ready to make it on his own and no longer feels he needs the old man. That's what we've seen unfold on Yawkey Way, and that's why the Theo deal is not done yet.
>
> Larry taught Theo too well and now he is looking in the mirror as he tries to hammer out a deal with the GM he made in his own image. Both are merely doing what they are trained to do. In Theo's case, he's doing what Larry trained him to do.
>
> What is alarming—for the future of the Sox franchise—is Theo's sudden need to distance himself from those who helped him rise to his position of power. Lucchino and Dr. Charles Steinberg are a pair of Red Sox executives who "discovered" Theo when he was a student at Yale. They picked him out of thousands of wannabe interns. They hired

him in Baltimore and then took him to San Diego with them. They held his hand and drove him places during his Wonder Years. They urged him to get his law degree. And when they set up stakes at Fenway Park, they fought vigorously to bring him home. A year later, when Billy Beane got cold feet, Lucchino turned to 28-year-old Theo and made him the (then) youngest GM in the history of baseball.

And now Theo "bristles at the notion of Steinberg and Lucchino taking credit for his success."

The agenda of Shaughnessy's article was clear: get Lucchino's side of the story out there, and smear a little dirt on Theo in the process. The last quote, the one that said Theo "bristles at the notion of Steinberg and Lucchino taking credit for his success," was a line from Shaughnessy's book. It wasn't a direct quote from Theo's mouth, it was Shaughnessy's opinion. In the column he admitted that the line was from his book, but the way it reads initially, it makes Theo sound like an ungrateful punk, which he sure as hell is not. Steinberg, now a member of the Los Angeles Dodgers' front office, said he and Theo remain in touch and are still "very close." Theo hasn't forgotten about Steinberg or any of the help he provided in Baltimore or San Diego.

Many felt that Lucchino had a hand in Shaughnessy's column, including Theo. He told Seth Mnookin, author of the 2006 book, *Feeding the Monster: How Money, Smarts, and Nerve Took a Team to the Top*, that he was "at peace" with his decision to accept the $4.5 million offer... until Shaughnessy's piece went to press. The column sucked the wind out of Theo. It was a sucker punch from someone, and some speculated that Steinberg was the wizard behind the curtain of condescension. But Theo's actions suggested otherwise; would he really have resigned if Steinberg was behind the column? Steinberg was vice president of Public Affairs; he wasn't a power broker in the Red Sox's organization. Theo and Steinberg had always had a personal understanding, and the two could have handled the situation quietly, behind closed doors.

Lucchino, on the other hand, was president and CEO. A shot from him was a shot from the top, and Theo worked much more closely with Lucchino than he did with Steinberg. This was a man that Theo would have to look in the eye every day for the next three years, and it would be nearly impossible for him to do so after the *Globe* piece. There may have also been a sense of embarrassment for Theo—the column painted a picture of him as childish, hubristic, and brash. It also implied that he was lucky to be general manager in the first place, and should be kissing Lucchino's feet and thanking him for his grace on a daily basis.

It was the classic battle of the old versus the young. Lucchino and Shaughnessy had been around, "seen it all," and weren't about to let a 31-year-old hot shot continue to walk the streets of Boston with a halo above his head, and a pair of wings attached to his back. Shaughnessy didn't do a great job of disguising his intentions, either. He wrote:

> Let's start with Theo being a "baseball guy" while Larry is a lawyer with a lofty title (CEO). Granted, Epstein is a student of the game, but it's a mistake to say he knows more about baseball than Lucchino or anyone else in the Red Sox baseball operation. Theo is 31 years old and did not play baseball past high school. He spent four years at Yale and three years at law school. That hardly leaves time for much more than rotisserie league scouting. He can read the data and has a horde of trusty, like-minded minions, but we're not talking about a lifetime of beating the bushes and scouting prospects.

Wow. So because Theo was young, and didn't have as much professional experience as Lucchino, he couldn't possibly know more about evaluating players and putting together a team? Was Theo's short-lived playing career the best insult Shaughnessy had? Many baseball executives lack professional playing experience; that doesn't mean they can't make the correct baseball operational decisions. Theo had already proven himself with a championship in his second year on the job; his high school baseball statistics didn't seem to matter to Shaughnessy after the '04

World Series, did they?

The bitterness was apparent—Lucchino had been a high-ranking front officer in baseball since 1979 and was a part of only one World Series champion (the '83 Orioles) before the 2004 Red Sox; Theo had been a GM for only three years, and already had a World Series title to add to his rapidly-expanding resume. The better years of Lucchino's life were behind him, and Shaughnessy felt his pain. He leapt to his ally's side, leaving Theo in a pit of fire.

Theo was understandably more upset with Lucchino than Shaughnessy, but his gripe with Shaughnessy remained legitimate. Bill Simmons called Shaughnessy's piece a "hideous mentor-protégé column that was clearly meant to put [Theo] in his place," and the overwhelming consensus agreed with him. The worst part was that, just a year earlier, Theo helped Shaughnessy put another feather in the cap of his career with *Reversing the Curse*. An overwhelmingly private man, Theo decided to talk to Shaughnessy for hours, giving away information about his family and behind-the-scenes activity with the Red Sox. Theo was a key part of *Reversing the Curse's* success, and this was how Shaughnessy chose to repay him.

According to Mnookin, after reading Shaughnessy's column, Theo sent an e-mail to John Henry.

"I have a huge pit in my stomach," Theo wrote, "but it's nowhere near as big a pit as I'd have if I'd already signed a contract."

With that, Theo was gone. And yet, somehow, amidst

all the drama, controversy, and conflict, he left his fans with smiles on their faces when he left Fenway in the now-infamous gorilla suit.

Sure, there was necessity involved in Theo's unusual maneuver, but its comedic value cannot be ignored. He was raised in a family where wit and humor were embraced, and none embraced comedy more than his father, Leslie. When the media was frenzying about the Red Sox's decision to name Theo the youngest GM in baseball history, Leslie said, "What's all the fuss about? When Alexander the Great was Theo's age, he was general manager of the world." (Leslie's shenanigans would come into play later in Theo's life, only then they'd have a more profound effect.)

The gorilla suit was later sold at the annual Hot Stove Cool Music charity concert, an event spearheaded by the aforementioned Peter Gammons. Jim Holzman, the owner of the Ace Ticket broker business in Brookline, Massachusetts—Theo's hometown—dropped $11,000 on the ape attire.

So in a time of intense turmoil, Theo was able to make a smart, but light-hearted move. It wasn't a trade, signing or any other transaction—it was a move to protect his privacy as he entered the next stage of his life, a stage away from Yawkey Way, away from Fenway Park, and away from the Boston Red Sox, the team he had adored throughout his life.

Part I: First Love Never Dies

When you love something, walking away from it can be one of the most painful experiences in the world. Sometimes we move on and never look back, but other times it's impossible to stay the course. Somewhere along the journey in the opposite direction, there's an about face.

Theo Epstein loved baseball, and loved his hometown team. Stepping away from both, it was no surprise that he had separation anxiety. He couldn't shake the Red Sox—his players, coworkers, memories, and triumphs—so he decided to swallow his pride and double back on his decision to resign. It was less than three months after his shocking farewell.

On January 24, 2006, Theo Epstein ran back to his love, and embraced her with a long hug. John Henry, Tom Werner, and Larry Lucchino welcomed back their general manager, and for good measure, they added executive vice president to his title. What had been a war in late October had become a nauseating love fest. This story had "chick flick" written all over it.

"On behalf of all of the partners as well as the entire management of the Boston Red Sox, I can tell you that we are exceedingly happy to have Theo returning as general manager," Henry said in a pre-organized statement. "Despite the attempts of some to portray Theo's return as a win for someone and a loss for someone else, this is a win-win situation."

Even the man who was the immediate cause of Theo's resignation was spewing the lovey-dovey, mushy stuff.

"The Red Sox are a stronger, deeper, bolder, and more effective organization now that Theo Epstein has rejoined us as general manager," Lucchino said, "and that strength, depth, boldness, and effectiveness will lead to successful baseball teams in the years ahead."

All of the comments from the Red Sox execs, including those from Theo, reflected the water under the bridge mentality. Theo said he stayed in touch with the three wise men during his hiatus, and that over time they were able to work out their philosophical differences. The funny thing was, the public statements—their first new order of business as a unit—showed that they *weren't* on the same page… not yet, at least.

"As Theo said in his press conference on November 2, and as we have all repeated, there never was a power struggle between Larry and Theo," Henry said. "It was simply mythology. I can assure you as we move forward that Larry's role has not changed at all, and no general manager in baseball could ask for more autonomy than Theo has. This has never been an issue for us—only in the media."

Henry said, "There never was a power struggle between Larry and Theo."

And Theo said: "As accomplished as the Red Sox were last October, there were fundamental disagreements among members of upper management with respect to organizational philosophy, approaches and priorities. This lack of a shared vision, plus the stress of a far-too-public negotiation, strained some relationships, including mine with Larry Lucchino."

Lack of a shared vision? Strained relationships? Sounds like a power struggle.

Lucchino followed suit: "The 14-year relationship between Theo and me, and the passage of time over the last three months, have helped to put behind us the friction that developed during last year's negotiations."

Friction?

The battle for power didn't seem to be a "myth," as Henry described it. Theo and Lucchino made it seem like anything but. If the three were suspects in a murder trial, they would struggle to get their stories straight. In this case, Henry would have been the one to take the fall.

Nonetheless, Red Sox Nation was ecstatic about the return of their young mastermind. Ben Cherington and Jed Hoyer, the duo named co-GMs in Theo's absence, returned to their positions in Baseball Operations.

As Shakespeare once wrote, "All's well that ends well"—and so it did in the Red Sox's front office.

Part II: Building a Champion... Again

In 2005, the Red Sox were swept out of the opening round of the playoffs by the eventual World Series champion White Sox. Chicago embarrassed Boston by the score of 14-2 in game 1 of the best-of-five series, and then squeaked by with respective 5-4 and 5-3 victories in games 2 and 3. The Red Sox's season was over in the blink of a postseason eye. So what had changed in the year following Boston's dramatic return to World Series glory, after 86 years of failure?

The 2004 team had it all. Most famously, it had the ability to battle back and persevere when faced with elimination. But there was no such fight this time around; Boston couldn't scratch or claw its way to a single win over Chicago.

Was it a hangover from the grueling uphill battle that was the 2004 season? Or maybe the old sports cliché, "It's always more difficult to repeat," reared its ugly head. Both may have played a minimal role, but the Red Sox's front office knew what the biggest problem was: their roster had holes as deep as a 3-0 deficit against the Yankees in the American League Championship Series. They were massive holes, and yet, holes that could be filled.

Boston's most glaring weakness was in the starting pitching department. Theo decided not to break the bank on Pedro Martinez at the end of the 2004 season, and offered the surefire Hall of Famer a measly three-year contract worth $30 million. Pedro scoffed at the deal and went on to sign a more lucrative, four-year deal with the New York Mets. Red Sox Nation mourned the loss of Pedro, but Theo cut ties with the aging right-hander at exactly the right time. Pedro has since been an extreme disappointment in New York, batting injuries and performing poorly for the Mets.

While the decision to let Pedro walk was the correct one in the long run, his short-term replacement, righty Matt Clement, proved to be one of the worst acquisitions of Theo's career. In December of 2004, Theo inked Clement to a three-year deal worth $25.5 million. A three-year contract wouldn't normally be considered "short term," but Clement went on to appear in just 12 games in 2006, and miss the entire 2007 season after surgery on his labrum and rotator cuff.

Heading into the '05-06 off-season, Theo had six possible starting pitchers—Clement (pre-injury), Curt Schilling, Tim Wakefield, Bronson Arroyo, David Wells, and Jonathan Papelbon—none of whom came with a guarantee of success in 2006.

Schilling's severe ankle troubles that began with a retinaculum tear in 2004, forced him into the bullpen in

2005. His ankle couldn't withstand the strain of lengthy outings as a starter, which forced Clement into the No. 1 spot in the rotation.

Clement had always featured a good fastball and electric slider, but his control and command issues made him nothing more than a middle-of-the-rotation guy throughout his career. He didn't belong at the apex of an American League staff, and Boston's opposition knew it. Clement was the hurler on the hill for 14-2 beat down at the hands of the White Sox in game 1 of the '05 playoffs. Chicago knocked him out, and then stomped him for good measure. Clement surrendered seven hits, three homers, and eight runs in just 3 1/3 innings.

In a worst-case scenario, Clement would be Theo's No. 2 starter in '06. He'd be joined in the rotation by Wakefield, Wells, and a fresher, more durable Schilling. Schilling was scheduled to resume the role of staff ace, meaning the youngster Papelbon would have to wait his turn. Arroyo would occupy the final starting spot—or so it seemed.

Theo's potential rotation looked solid, but not spectacular. However, it wouldn't be "Theo's rotation" for long, as he stunned the baseball world and stepped down, leaving the keys with a starting five of Lucchino, Ben Cherington, Jed Hoyer, Bill Lajoie, and Craig Shipley.

"When Theo left, what it came down to was four people running the club," Shipley said. "Jed spent most of his time in Boston, I spent a lot of time traveling and working on potential deals, Ben was running the farm system, and Bill was special assistant evaluating players."

The fearsome foursome was forced to confront a couple of lingering questions: could Schilling be trusted to return to his 2004 form, and would the Red Sox be good enough to win a World Series with Clement as their No. 2 starter?

Those questions were answered in late November of 2005, when the Red Sox acquired starting pitcher Josh Beckett, an intimidating 6-foot-4 fireballer from the Florida Marlins. The Sox also received veteran third baseman Mike Lowell and right-handed reliever Guillermo Mota in the trade.

Beckett was just 25 years old at the time of the deal, but already sported a World Series ring on his finger. Beckett was named World Series Most Valuable Player in 2003, when his Marlins defeated the New York Yankees in six games. He picked up two wins in the series, including a complete-game shutout in the decisive game 6. Beckett dominated the Yankees with 95-to-98 mph fastball, a vicious overhand curve, and an effective change-up (if it can still be considered a change-up at 90 to 91 mph).

So the Sox picked up a young ace with incredible stuff, postseason experience, and a track record of big-time success against the Yankees. It was a spectacular trade for Boston's front office, the question was, who was behind it? The deal was so spectacular that speculators suggested Theo's involvement.

On Thanksgiving Day of 2005, Lucchino made calls to Hoyer, Lajoie, and Shipley. It was time for them to come to a decision on the Beckett trade. The offer was on the table, and the Marlins were looking for a final answer. Initially, the decision was a unanimous "yes." But at the last minute, one man changed his vote.

Hoyer was concerned about Lowell's health and nervous about parting ways with Boston's talented prospects. He switched over to "no," despite the team physician's satisfaction with Lowell's physical condition. Even if he was healthy, Hoyer believed that Lowell's better days were behind him.

Lajoie disagreed. He scouted Lowell often in '04, and felt they had "never seen a guy hit into tougher luck." Lowell hit line drives consistently and displayed the ability to hit with power to the opposite field. Despite the nagging injuries, Lajoie said Lowell continued to have a quality approach at the dish and never quit at any point in the year. With good reason—he "knew what Theo wanted"—Lajoie believed Lowell had at least two or three strong seasons left in the tank.

Lucchino ultimately sided with Lajoie, Shipley, and Cherington. With the move, the Sox boasted two aces at the top of their rotation, Schilling and Beckett, with Clement, Wakefield, and Wells filling out the three, four, and five spots. With the pocket aces in hand, their rotation's infrastructure closely resembled that of the 2004 team (with Schilling and Pedro), and the 2001 World Series champion Arizona Diamondbacks, who flaunted both Schilling and eventual Hall of Famer Randy Johnson.

Still, the Sox had to give to get Beckett. The Marlins demanded that Boston eat up the remainder of Lowell's contract, two years worth $18 million. Lowell struggled mightily in 2005, hitting just .236 with eight homers in 500 at bats, and his body appeared to be breaking down. Making $9 million per season, the Sox were essentially forced to make Lowell their everyday third baseman in 2006, an idea that certainly didn't bother Lajoie.

Penciling Lowell into the lineup on a daily basis meant goodbye to Bill Mueller. Mueller was one of Theo's most beloved players, the starting third baseman on the World Series team, and the American League's batting champion in 2003 (.326). For a sabermetrician like Theo, Mueller was a dream come true. From 2003 to 2005, Mueller's on-base percentages were .398, .365, and .369 respectively. In addition, Mueller's slugging percentages were strong at .540, .446, and .430. But notice the decline in the slugging numbers, surely something the Red Sox's brass, including Theo, recognized. Mueller's home run totals also declined consistently over that three-year period, so as much as it may have hurt Theo to see Mueller go, the transition to the Lowell era may not have been as difficult as it looked from the outside.

Lowell had an on-base percentage of .340 or better for five consecutive seasons, from 2000 to 2004. Maybe '05 was a fluke. Maybe Lowell would be productive again in '06.

Not only did the Marlins force-feed Lowell's contract to the Red Sox, they also received Boston's prized prospect in the Beckett deal, sensational shortstop Hanley Ramirez. Ramirez was an exceptional young talent, signed in 2000 as an amateur free agent by Dan Duquette, Theo's predecessor. (Although, Mike Port did work as "interim GM" between Duquette and Theo). Interestingly enough, none of Theo's major draftees—namely Papelbon, Dustin Pedroia, and Jacoby Ellsbury—were shipped to Florida in the blockbuster. Coincidence?

The jury is still out.

The Beckett and Lowell for Ramirez deal will be remembered as one of the true "win-wins" in baseball history, as Beckett and Lowell have made incredible contributions to the Red Sox since their arrival, and Ramirez has been simultaneously breathtaking and revitalizing for the Marlins. His flash and natural ability are attractive to fans, and his exuberance and statistical excellence bring energy to a sometimes-lifeless franchise.

In Theo's absence, the Sox's rotation was set and a new third baseman was added to the mix. It was time for Boston to address its bullpen, but behind the scenes, controversy was brewing in the front office.

During Theo's hiatus, Lucchino was forced to rely on the rest of his Baseball Operations department. One day prior to Theo's resignation, Lajoie stepped down for health reasons. Lucchino lost both his top dog and most experienced baseball mind in the span of two days. When it was clear that Theo wouldn't be returning, Lucchino called Lajoie for help. After getting calls from Lucchino a few days in a row, Lajoie suggested that—rather than conduct business over the phone—he should return to Boston on a segmented basis.

Lucchino was relieved; he drew up a contract that guaranteed quarterly payments and tentatively put Lajoie in charge. If Theo left for good, the general manager position was Lajoie's for the taking.

Lajoie said he and Shipley were largely responsible for the Beckett deal, as well as the moves that brought Mark Loretta and Andy Marte to Boston. And yet, after the winter meetings, John Henry named Cherington and Hoyer co-GMs.

Lucchino was surprised by the announcement; Lajoie and Shipley were taken aback. The two had done the vast majority of the work in Theo's absence, and understandably, it upset them to be overlooked. But before things could get really messy, Theo returned to save the day, or at least try to.

After officially being restored to the role of general manager, Theo put in a call to Lajoie, who had left town after Cherington and Hoyer took the reins. Theo wasn't beating around the bush.

"Bill, we want you to stay on the staff," he pleaded.

But it was too late. Lajoie felt that if he returned, he'd be forced to choose between Theo and Lucchino. Lajoie said Lucchino had nothing to do with Cherington and

Hoyer being named co-GMs; regardless, Larry spent most of his time with Henry and Werner. Being with Larry often meant being with Henry, and Lajoie wanted little to do with the latter. In the end, Lajoie didn't want to betray Larry or Theo, so he gave his notice, and left town.

Theo would miss Lajoie, a man whom he trusted and had great respect for. But there was no time to dwell; the Red Sox had to address their messy bullpen situation—and quickly.

Theo had a closer in Keith Foulke, but there was little faith in the soft-tossing righty heading into the 2006 season. Foulke was a Godsend in 2004, taking over for converted starter Byung-Hyun Kim, and posting a 2.17 ERA with 32 saves. He battled through a number of difficult jams in the postseason, and completed the Red Sox's World Series sweep of the Cardinals by fielding a comebacker off the bat of shortstop Edgar Renteria (who thought "if you can't beat 'em, join 'em," and signed with Boston shortly after the series.) Renteria proceeded to become a major disappointment as a member of the Sox in 2005.

But Renteria wasn't the only disappointing Red Sock in 2005. Foulke lost his touch, and hit rock bottom. He battled knee problems throughout the season, and was eventually forced into surgery. Foulke finished with a catastrophic 5.91 ERA and only 15 saves. His knees were part of the problem, seemingly contributing to the decreased velocity of his fastball. Foulke had never been known as a flamethrower—particularly in comparison to elite, gas-pumping closers—but was able to reach 92 to 93 mph in the past. In 2005, he was lucky to scrape 90 mph. His fastball was consistently in the 87-to-89 range.

And yet, velocity had never been the key to Foulke's success. He was always noted for his command and a deceivingly filthy change-up. While the decreased velocity was a concern for Foulke, his biggest issue in '05 was spotty command. A pitcher who doesn't locate his mid-to-upper 80s fastball is a pitcher who gets hammered.

After a terrible season and tricky surgery, Theo and friends had the right to be worried about Foulke in '06. The Sox contemplated converting him into a setup man, an idea that threw him into the mix with veteran right-handers Mike Timlin and Julian Tavarez, who was signed away from the Cardinals shortly before Theo's return. Arroyo, the starter pushed out of the rotation by Beckett, would join the bullpen. He pitched well in a few relief opportunities during the '04 playoffs.

But who would close? The situation was beginning to look more and more like the 2003 disaster, only this time Theo planned to have a closer... he just wasn't sure who it would be.

Late in spring training, Theo took Arroyo out of the equation by trading him to the Reds for outfielder Wily Mo Pena. Theo realized a few seasons earlier that right fielder Trot Nixon could not be considered an everyday player, due to struggles against left-handed pitching. Gabe Kapler was still around as an option against lefties, but

Pena offered more power and promise. Theo's pull of the transaction trigger left Foulke, Timlin, Tavarez, and former Seattle Mariners' starter Joel Pineiro in a four-way battle for the closer position.

Enter Jonathan Papelbon. At 6-foot-4 and over 200 pounds of intensity and passion for the game, Theo selected Papelbon as a starting pitcher in the fourth round of the '03 amateur draft. The big right-hander had a reputation as a fierce competitor, and threw 34 innings for the Sox in 2005, going 3-1 with a 2.65 ERA.

With Beckett on board, and Schilling back in the rotation, Papelbon was the odd man out. The Arroyo trade helped him climb one rung up the organizational ladder, but as a starting pitcher, he remained a backup plan.

Boston's brass felt that Papelbon would be wasted in Triple-A, not contributing to the major league club until someone got injured, so they decided to let him pitch in relief. With a 94-to-98 mph fastball, a hard splitter, and decent slider, Papelbon would be a handful for the opposition in a short-term situation.

"Paps" was untouchable in the preseason, and as Opening Day rapidly approached, there were whispers about him winning the closer's job. The obvious concerns were that he was just 25 years old at the time, and his experience at the major league level was limited. But then again, Beckett was only 25, and yet *he* was expected to be one of the anchors of the rotation. Was a youth movement, which started with Theo's promotion to general manager in 2003, completely underway?

On Opening Day of the 2006 season, David Ortiz, Manny Ramirez, Trot Nixon, and Jason Varitek were the holdovers from the '05 starting lineup. Kevin Youkilis, long considered one of the most polished prospects in Boston's minor league system, would finally get his chance as an everyday player. Youkilis took over at first base, despite spending the majority of his minor league career at the hot corner. As a primary bench player for the Sox in 2005, "Youk" played a few innings at first, and performed more than adequately.

Predecessor Kevin Millar had packed his bags for the division-rival Baltimore Orioles, and Sox management wanted to avoid moving Ortiz from his comfortable DH position. Everything considered, Youk was a near no-brainer at first. He was a favorite of Theo's, regardless of the fact that he was drafted prior to the Epstein regime.

Famously, in Michael Lewis' *Moneyball: The Art of Winning an Unfair Game*—the book that placed a piercing spotlight on Billy Beane's general managerial style— Youkilis was referred to as the "Greek God of Walks." Sabermetricians like Theo and Beane place immense value on walks and on-base percentage, and Youkilis worked the count as well as anyone. So much so, that Beane tried feverishly to acquire Youkilis from the Sox while he was in the minors. Theo wasn't having it. He saw what Beane saw in Youkilis, and made sure to strengthen his hold on Sir Walk-a-Lot.

At second base, veteran journeyman Mark Loretta was set to take over for Mark Bellhorn. Bellhorn was another sabermetric favorite of Theo's, but his strikeout total cut too deeply into his on-base percentage in '05. Loretta was widely regarded as a "professional hitter," a right-hander with the ability to get the count in his favor, hit to all fields, and put up a solid batting average. He was a safe choice as a replacement, albeit one with a ceiling.

Lowell was in place of Mueller at third, and Renteria was supplanted at short; just days after returning, Theo signed slick-fielding shortstop Alex Gonzalez to a one-year deal worth $3 million. Gonzalez wasn't in Renteria's league offensively, but was arguably the premier defensive shortstop in baseball. Gonzalez was as consistent as they come on the routine plays, with the ability to make exceptional plays, and make them regularly. Renteria, on the other hand, gave Red Sox fans a collective migraine with his league-worst 30 errors in '05.

In the outfield, Manny manned his customary left field position, and Nixon patrolled right. The change, and it was a big one, came in center field. Millar had left for a division rival in the Orioles, but Johnny Damon took betrayal to a whole 'nother level when he jumped ship to a different division rival… the New York Yankees. Damon stabbed each and every member of Red Sox Nation in the back when he inked a four-year contract worth $52 million to join the Evil Empire.

Right around the time of Theo's comeback, the Sox

addressed the hole in center field, or better yet, the hole in the hearts of Red Sox fans. Not only was Damon their primary center fielder and top baserunner—he was their leadoff man. Theo loved Damon's on-base ability, and his teammates loved his hustle and infectious attitude. On January 23, 2006, the Sox dealt popular third base prospect Andy Marte, catcher Kelly Shoppach, and reliever Guillermo Mota (who came over in the Beckett trade) to the Cleveland Indians for middle reliever David Riske, switch-hitting catcher Josh Bard, and a new centerfielder, Covelli Crisp. Covelli was and is better known as "Coco" Crisp.

Yup, like the cereal.

Coco was coming off his breakout season in Cleveland, where he hit .300 with 16 homers, 69 RBI, and 15 stolen bases, all out of the Indians' leadoff spot. Coco was young, aggressive, exciting, and versatile. A switch hitter with virtually unlimited range in the outfield, many were perplexed at Cleveland's decision to deal him. But the Indians had another franchise centerfielder waiting in the wings, sweet-stroking Grady Sizemore. To Cleveland's management, the future of their outfield was bright, while their third base situation was bleak. Marte was one of the most talked about third base prospects in years, so they jumped at the opportunity to inherit him from Boston.

Manager Terry Francona would plug Coco into the Opening Day leadoff spot, and hope—not expect—that he would mirror Damon's production and clubhouse impact. Damon's were big shoes to fill, and Coco was a little man at about 5'10", 170 lbs. The odds were against the cereal centerfielder.

Coco and Lowell were wild cards, but for the most part Theo's lineup was rock solid. His rotation looked promising with Schilling on the hill for the opener, and Wakefield, Beckett, Clement, and Wells to follow in that order.

With both the lineup and rotation organized, the bullpen was once again the question mark. Schilling began the season with seven solid innings of work, surrendering only two runs on five hits at the Texas Rangers' home park. The Ballpark in Arlington is notoriously one of the best hitters' parks in baseball, making Schilling's success all the more encouraging. Concerns about the durability of his ankle were dismissed, at least momentarily.

With a 7-2 lead to begin the bottom of the eighth inning, Francona looked to Theo's bullpen. He summoned Papelbon, a move that suggested that the youngster would *not* be the team's closer to open the year. Closers almost always appear in the ninth inning, even in a non-save situation. Handing the ball to Papelbon in the eighth implied that he would be one of Francona's primary setup men. But who would close?

Papelbon looked sharp in his season debut, retiring the side in order and striking out one. Though he had been a starting pitcher throughout his minor league career, Papelbon's demeanor was that of a closer—focused, intense, unshakable. After sitting the Rangers down one-two-three, he walked off the mound as if it were nothing. He expected success, and many in the Red Sox's organization were impressed with his confidence. Theo was among those impressed. But then again, he had always admired Papelbon—he did, of course, draft him in the fourth round of the 2003 draft.

After Papelbon's easy inning, Francona called for Foulke in the ninth. The Sox's five-run lead made it a non-save situation for Foulke, but the fact that he followed Papelbon in the bullpen suggested a return to the closer's role. Foulke struggled in his first outing, letting up two clean hits, including a rocket double off the bat of Rangers' right fielder Kevin Mench. Centerfielder Laynce Nix eventually plated Mench with a sacrifice fly. Foulke retired the next batter, catcher Rod Barajas, for the final out of the game, an easy 7-3 win for the Sox.

Francona's hand had been revealed: Papelbon would pave the way for Foulke. Foulke was a train wreck in '05, but the Sox planned to pat him on the butt and throw him back into the fray in '06.

Or did they?

Two nights later, April 5, the Red Sox led 2-1 heading into the bottom of the ninth inning. They had taken on the chin the day before, losing by six runs in a 10-4 final. The Rangers were able to get to Wakefield, the crafty knuckleballer, early in the game. He tossed just 3 2/3 innings, and allowed seven earned runs.

So with the series tied at 1-1, and the Sox gripping tightly to a one-run lead, everyone expected Foulke to trot out of the bullpen for the ninth. Oddly enough, old country hardballer Mike Timlin had pitched in the eighth, not Papelbon.

When the door to the bullpen swung open, with the opening series of the season on the line, out came… Jonathan Papelbon.

Papelbon stormed to the hill and picked up the ball. Theo's draftee was pumped, there was no concealing it. But was Foulke hurt? He didn't pitch in game 2 of the series, either. At the time, it didn't matter. With eyes glued to their television screens, members of Red Sox Nation everywhere scratched their heads. They wondered about Foulke, and wondered what their closer of the future had to offer.

Their questions were answered, and answered quickly.

Barajas led off the inning, and Papelbon mowed him down, striking him out swinging while featuring a blistering 96-to-97 mph heater. Nix followed in the order, and Papelbon overpowered him, inducing a short pop fly to left field.

Papelbon cruised past the first two hitters, but it remained a one-run game. One swing of the bat could tie it and leadoff hitter Brad Wilkerson strolled confidently up to the dish. Wilkerson was an unusual choice for the leadoff spot, known for drawing walks, but striking out a ton and hitting for a low average. Wilkerson was just another indication that the days of the speedy, little, bunt-and-slap leadoff hitters were coming to an end. His build was strong, and he had crushed 32 homers with the Expos in '04. With the speed of Papelbon's fastball, Wilkerson wouldn't have to hit it on the sweet spot to pop one out of the Ballpark in Arlington. Papelbon probably should have been careful with him, but...

He went right after him with the heat. Catcher and team captain Jason Varitek had confidence in Papelbon's velocity and tenacity. Papelbon blew Wilkerson away, striking him out swinging to complete a one-two-three ninth in his very first save situation.

Theo was happy, but not surprised. He had seen Papelbon's potential long before April 5, 2006, a day that signaled the beginning of a new era at the back of Boston's bullpen. Foulke was a workhorse for the Sox in '04 when they needed him most, but Boston's management had rightfully determined that his days as a dominant closer were over.

"Nothing seems to shake this kid," said Francona of Papelbon's early season performance. "[But] we want to get Foulke back to the guy we want to go to in the ninth. I think our team is set up that if we do that, we're going to have a lights-out bullpen. As for Pap, there is no doubt in my mind that he will be a very good starter for us for a long time."

As usual, Francona said the right things to the media, not revealing the organization's cards, and showing respect to the veteran Foulke. But after watching Papelbon do his thing for a couple of weeks, Theo and Francona found it easy to abandon their originally conservative plan. Papelbon was just too good to demote. With the game on the line, the ball would be his—permanently.

This type of decision exemplifies the fortune-changing organizational upgrades made during Theo Epstein's Red Sox reign. Foulke was under a $21 million contract, while Papelbon was making slightly over $335,000—close to the league minimum—and yet the Sox said screw the money, and went with their gut. Credit Theo for trusting his team with a manager willing to make critical, last minute changes on the field, and answer media questions about those changes off the field. Francona has done a fantastic job for Theo, from day one of the 2004 season to the present.

Papelbon went on to have one of the greatest seasons in the history of relief pitching. He finished the year with an ERA under 1.00, a statistic totally unheard of in the era of small ballparks, juiced baseballs, and muscle-bound, machine-like hitters. Papelbon's official ERA was 0.92; he allowed only seven earned runs in slightly over 68 innings of work. An average of one strikeout per inning is considered a superb rate, and Papelbon fanned 75 in his 68 innings. Theo drafted himself a lights-out closer without even realizing it. Papelbon was a keeper, and Theo could do no wrong.

Well, not exactly. The '06 season proved disastrous for

the Red Sox and their faithful. Boston finished a respectable 10 games over .500, with an 86-76 record, but Theo and company weren't looking for respectable, they were looking for another World Series title. Things went so wrong that the Sox failed to finished *third* in the American League East. The Toronto Blue Jays, constructed by Theo's buddy J.P. Ricciardi, finished second behind the hated Yankees.

Swept out of the playoffs in 2005, short of the postseason in 2006—what had gone wrong? Was Theo allowing the Red Sox to begin down another long path of failure?

That remained to be seen, but the injury bug undoubtedly contributed to Boston's struggles in '06. Varitek appeared in just 103 games after playing in 133 in 2005, Crisp played in 105 after 145, Manny 130 after 152, and Alex Gonzalez 111 after 130.

On the pitching staff, Wakefield threw in only 23 games after appearing in 33 the year before, and Clement was lost for the season during the first quarter of the year.

Regardless, Theo would have to answer for Crisp and Gonzalez. His cabinet members had helped him usher the duo into Boston during the offseason, and both were disappointments in '06.

Theo was a devout follower of his special advisor to Baseball Operations, Bill James. Beginning in the late 1970s and ending in the late '80s, James wrote a series of *Baseball Abstracts* that revealed his original thoughts about player evaluation, lineup and bullpen construction, defensive value, and game strategy, among other things.

In his 1982 *Abstract*, James talked about players who approached baseball as if it were football. That is, players who exert *too* much effort (yes, he believes there is such a thing) laying out for everything, crashing into walls, and diving head first when a simple pop-up slide would suffice. James said such players were poor investments, especially when you consider the lengthy 162-game major league schedule. Season-ending injuries were always a concern with that breed of ballplayers, and James generally felt that they weren't worth the hassle.

The '06 Red Sox had a player who fit into that dubious category… his name was Coco Crisp. Coco had always displayed intense passion for the game, what James may have considered intensity to a fault. Coco was known for making eye-popping diving catches in centerfield, but was also a risk-taker. Often he would dive for balls out of his reach, causing hard, unnecessary contact with the ground.

And yet, even with James on the staff, the Sox made the move for Crisp. Not surprisingly (to James, at least) Coco suffered finger, hand, and shoulder injuries during the ensuing season. The hand injury cost him 42 games in the first half, and he missed the final 10 games of the year due to the sprained finger. Coco scattered five other DNPs throughout the season, most of which were a result of his nagging shoulder problem.

The injuries must've affected Coco's performance because his batting average dropped 36 points from 2005, and his on-base percentage dipped 28 points to an unimpressive .317. Coco failed to bolster Theo's reputation in '06. Missing the playoffs made his acquisition look even worse.

Beckett also tanked in his first Red Sox season. However, his struggles weren't injury-related. Beckett had an unnerving history of arm trouble, but it was his teammates who contracted the injury bug in '06.

Beckett's problems were in pitch selection and execution. He pitched to an abnormally high 5.01 ERA for the year, after finishing in the 3's the previous three seasons. He had never had an ERA above 4.10 before 2006.

The consensus was that Beckett had fallen in love with his fastball, in part because of an ongoing battle to command his devastating curveball. When Beckett was unable to find the handle on his curve with the Marlins, his mid-to-upper 90s fastball was enough to shut down National League lineups. But in the American League each lineup has an extra, professional bat in the person of the designated hitter. At times when Beckett may have faced the opposing pitcher or a low-level pinch hitter in the NL, he was pitching to another solid, everyday player in the AL. Big difference.

On the bright side, the big fella was able to battle for 16 victories. Theo and the rest of Boston's management assumed Beckett needed time to adjust to American League lineups and the friendly offensive confines of Fenway Park. Adjustments he could make, or so they hoped.

Those hopes were revealed after one of Beckett's better performances in '06: eight innings, four hits, no runs, and a win against Kansas City on July 19. Francona met with the media for his customary post-game press conference that night, and dropped a quiet bomb (if there is such a thing) on his interviewers.

"[Beckett] threw the ball so well that I think Theo just gave him a three-year deal," Francona said. "If he pitches good next time, he might get six years."

Chuckles could be heard throughout the room. Terry's a funny guy.

"No, I'm serious," he clarified.

Cue the raised eyebrows and confused looks.

"Wait a second, are you serious?" one baffled reporter blurted out.

Oddly enough, Terry wasn't joking. His delivery was so matter-of-fact that it took everyone by surprise. Theo had quietly inked his intimidating right-hander to a deal through 2009—three years, $30 million, with a $12 million team option for a fourth season.

It was another savvy investment, no doubt, by Theo. However, '06 was still a down year for Beckett and the Sox. Heading into the off-season, it was up to Theo to decide if the injuries were ultimately to blame for that down year. It wasn't all bad, as the Sox were able to develop Papelbon into an exceptional closer; young lefty starter Jon Lester showed promise after being promoted from Triple-A; Schilling was able to make 31 starts and won 15 games;

Lowell surprised everyone by appearing in 153 games and hitting 20 homers; and David Ortiz had another monster season as the team's DH.

Theo's off-season activity suggested that he was somewhere in between. He made four key acquisitions, but also stuck with his guns at many positions. He liked what he had in place, but to be safe brought in some heavy artillery.

The Red Sox's headliner of the '06-07 off-season was Japanese sensation Daisuke Matsuzaka. Commonly referred to as "Dice-K," Matsuzaka was the most dominant pitcher overseas. He was a No. 1 draft pick of the Seibu Lions in 1998, and was named Pacific League Rookie of the Year just a season later. Dice-K received the 2001 Sawamura Award (the Japanese equivalent of the Cy Young) by baffling hitters with his mythical "gyroball" and blowing others away with smoke.

Dice-K's Japanese baseball credentials were all well and good, but it was in the '06 World Baseball Classic that he mesmerized major league hitters, coaches, and executives. In a tournament including loaded teams from the United States and Dominican Republic, Japan shocked everyone by winning it all with a 10-6 victory over Cuba. Dice-K was named tournament MVP after allowing only two runs in 13 total innings of work.

Following the World Baseball Classic, the Dice-K sweepstakes was underway in America. The other big names on the free agent market were left-hander Barry

Zito, formerly of the Athletics, and righty Jason Schmidt, an ex-Giant. Theo looked past the two proven major leaguers, and gazed preeminently at Matsuzaka. With the shrewd, cunning, money-hungry Scott Boras as his agent, Theo knew that Matsuzaka would command a hefty chunk of change—as hefty, or heftier than Rich Garces' belly (that's huge).

The Yankees, Dodgers, Giants, and Astros were all said to be in the market for a big-time free agent hurler. Red Sox owner John Henry was prepared for Theo to dig a bit deeper into his wallet than normal.

In December of '06, Theo made a $51.11 million offer for the rights to Daisuke Matsuzaka. Basically, it was $51 million to talk to Dice-K. There was no guarantee that the Japanese gyroballer would sign with the Sox. However, with a baseball mind as calculating as Theo's, he must've received assurances from Boras. Was Dice-K good enough for Theo to risk wasting $51 million?

Of course not. After Hideki Irabu, Kasuhisa Ishii, Masato Yoshii, and the rest of the failed Asian pitcher experiments, knowledgeable MLB executives had to be somewhat skeptical of Matsuzaka. Though, to Dice-K's credit, he received rave reviews from the big league hitters that faced him in the World Baseball Classic. Most batters cited his deceptive motion and array of breaking pitches as strengths. With a fastball that reached 96 mph with some regularity, Dice-K seemed to be more of a power pitcher than his Japanese predecessors in Major League Baseball.

Regardless, once Theo acquired the rights to Dice-K, he fully expected to sign him. His expectations were met on December 14, 2006, when Matsuzaka inked a six-year contract to play for the Boston Red Sox, worth $52 million.

"Today, what we're really doing is announcing the signing of a national treasure," said Theo at the press conference. "Dice-K is unique as a pitcher. We understand his importance in Japan. We know what he represents."

With the deal finalized, Boras had cleaned up once again: a grand total $103.1 million left the possession of the Red Sox in the negotiations. But in Theo's estimation, it was money well spent. Dice-K would join Schilling, Beckett, and Wakefield in Boston's rotation, giving them four quality starters.

The fifth starter should have been Lester, but in a twisted and heartbreaking turn of events the 22-year-old lefty was diagnosed a rare form of blood cancer known as non-Hodgkins lymphoma. Lester began treatment, dimming his bright future in baseball. The Sox would miss him in the clubhouse and on the field, and Theo was forced to replace him in the rotation. (Lester would eventually beat cancer and make a dramatic return to the Sox, late in the '07 season.)

Believing in the strength of their top four starters, Sox management penciled the veteran Julian Tavarez into the fifth and final spot. After a couple of excellent seasons as a setup man in St. Louis, he struggled in '06 as a member of Boston's relief core. Tavarez had been an effective start-ing pitcher in the past, particularly with the Florida Mar-lins, so Theo and crew figured they'd give him a shot. If he failed, they'd call up one of their young guns, possibly 2005 first-round pick Clay Buchholz. Papelbon was ini-tially supposed to return to his comfort zone as a starter, but late in spring training he decided it would be best for the club if he remained closer.

Theo wanted to avoid chasing another free agent starter because he had already broken the bank on a short-stop and right fielder. Throw those two contracts on top of Matsuzaka's $103.1 million, and it was time for Theo to give Henry's check-signing hand a rest.

Boston's new shortstop was Julio Lugo, a player who spent time with both the Dodgers and Devil Rays in '06. The skinny, 165-pound middle infielder had surprising pop—his lean frame didn't suggest the double-digit home run totals that he amassed in 2000, '01, '03, and '06.

Lugo's defensive skills were highly regarded. He was quick to both his glove and back-hand side, with a strong enough arm to make the throws in the hole. His explosive base running was a plus, and his on-base percentage was consistently in the .330 range.

On December 6, 2006, Theo signed Lugo to a four-year deal worth $36 million. He could be looked at as the median between Boston's previous two shortstops, Alex Gonzalez and Edgar Renteria. Lugo was a more dangerous hitter than Gonzalez, but an inferior fielder. Contrarily, he provided better defense than Renteria, with less offensive punch. Lugo gave Theo and Francona another option for the leadoff spot, just in case Coco Crisp continued struggling in '07.

Just a few hours prior to the Lugo signing, Theo put an end to the Trot Nixon era in right field. In an acquisition that revealed Theo's excitement more than any other, he inked J.D. Drew to a five-year deal worth $70 million.

Drew had spent the previous nine seasons of his career in the National League, and was most recently a member of the Los Angeles Dodgers. Basically, he was everything Theo could ask for.

Drew was a left-handed hitter with pop, set to slide into the No. 5 spot in Francona's batting order, behind the big boys, Ortiz and Manny. Immediately after the signing, Theo talked about Drew and his new-look lineup.

"I think we ranked 30th out of 30 teams in No. 5-hole OPS [on-base percentage plus slugging] last year," Theo said. "It wasn't even close. We weren't even close to 29th. If you do even a conservative estimate of Drew's performance for us next year in Fenway Park, that goes I think to around sixth or seventh out of what you should expect from the five-hole in all of baseball. It takes away a real weakness—five-hole production. Another elite bat behind David and Manny and turns it into a strength."

Theo was ecstatic. Drew was a smooth player who always moved with a certain degree of fluidity and grace. He may have been penciled into the No. 5 spot, but he didn't fit the physical mold of the average No. 5 hitter. Many teams used a big man in the five-spot, a corner infielder or outfielder with raw size and power who would clog the bases when he got on, but that wasn't the case with Drew. At about 6'1" and 195 lbs, Drew was lean and athletic with good speed on the bases and in the outfield. Theo believed Drew would improve the Red Sox both offensively and defensively.

"Once he opted out of his contract, he became a real attraction for us, because in one player—sure, it's a large commitment—but in one player, we could address or help address two areas of real weakness, and that's hard to do sometimes," Theo said.

Theo couldn't hide his affinity for Drew's ability. He would often talk to the media after a significant transaction, but kept his comments to a minimum. Not this time. Theo went on and on about Drew.

"He really has a great swing for Fenway Park," Theo said. "When he pulls the ball and elevates the ball, it will certainly reach the bullpen. He's got plus raw power. The big dimensions in right field and even center field won't be a problem for him. If you look at his hit chart, those balls get out."

Theo continued.

"He has the ability to hit the ball to left field in the air on a pretty consistent basis. That's before he makes any adjustments in his approach. The left-field wall really rewards left-handed hitters who let the ball get deep and are confident in their hands and have the ability to go the other way. We certainly think he can do that, even more than he has in the past. Just with the approach he's taken in the past, it will reward him. We think there's more in there."

Like a kid at the candy store, right? Well, as much as Theo admired Drew, his new right fielder was far from perfect. As is the case with any big pick-up, Drew came to town accompanied by some question marks.

First and foremost, Drew had a reputation as one of the most injury-prone players in the bigs. In eight official seasons, Drew had never played in more than 146 games. In four different years, he played in less than 110 games. Even scarier, in 2005, just a season earlier, he finished with only 252 at bats in 72 games. Drew exemplified the true definition of "injury-prone" because, over time, he had missed games for a variety of different reasons. He had issues with his back, shoulder, ankle, wrist, and even knees—the latter being a common injury for older players who are breaking down. But Drew was only 31 years old; he couldn't be breaking down... could he?

Theo didn't seem to think so. He cited Drew's 146 games played in 2006 (a career high) as proof of his health. But the concerns about Drew stretched beyond spotty health. Various scouts and executives around the league questioned Drew's passion for the game, and many wondered if he had the heart and guts necessary to produce in the clutch. The fans and media didn't pressure Drew in

Los Angeles or Atlanta, but that could change quickly if he failed to come through in Boston.

With Atlanta, Drew hit a measly .200 in the 2004 National League Division Series against the Houston Astros. When it looked like he couldn't get any worse in the postseason, he hit .154 with the Dodgers in the '06 NLDS. Drew spent the majority of the '06 series against the Mets grounding out weakly to the right side of the infield and strolling quietly and contently back to the Dodger dugout. It didn't look like he cared about losing, and scouts took notice of the free-agent-to-be's attitude.

But Theo shrugged off the concerns about Drew's ability under pressure (or lack thereof), perhaps because clutch hitting couldn't be factored into sabermetrics. Sabermetrics is rooted primarily in statistics, and statistical analyses of clutch performance are largely subjective.

When evaluating Drew, the stat that jumped out at Theo was on-base percentage: .412 in 2005, .436 in 2004, and .374 in 2003. He and Bill James had to be drooling over the production possibilities with Drew following Ortiz and Manny. Arguably the second-favorite number of sabermetricians, slugging percentage, was also a statistical strength of Drew's. From '03 to '05 he slugged .512, .569, and .520 respectively. All aspects considered it was no surprise that Theo was an enthusiastic member of J.D. Drew fan club.

In Matsuzaka, Lugo, and Drew, Theo had three of his four impact acquisitions of the '06-07 off-season. The fourth flew under the radar, but it may have been the best signing of them all.

On November 30, 2006, Theo signed Japanese left-hander Hideki Okajima to a two-year deal worth a little over $2.5 million. At the time of the transaction, fans, analysts, and executives alike, believed Theo was laying the groundwork for a Matsuzaka signing. It wasn't a slight on Okajima's ability, but everyone seemed to view him as bait for Dice-K. Okajima was a fellow countryman of Matsuzaka's, and Dice K's potential transition to America could be aided by the presence of a Japanese-speaking teammate.

Theo said of the deal, "Certainly, we made this move today for Okajima san on [his] merits. He's going to be a valuable member of our bullpen. If we do end up with two Japanese pitchers, that certainly would help the assimilation process, not only on the field but off the field."

While Theo gave Okajima his due, he also seemed intrigued by the duo of Okajima and Matsuzaka. He said he was bringing in Okajima on his own merits, but it was difficult for anyone to believe him. One member of Theo's front office team felt the need to clarify the situation.

"Let's put this Hideki Okajima thing to rest," said Craig Shipley, vice president of International Scouting. "We don't acquire players so another player can be comfortable. We couldn't assume that we'd win the race for Matsuzaka, so the Okajima deal was entirely independent of Dice-K's."

Okajima was very experienced in Japanese professional baseball, having pitched 11 years for the Yomiuri Giants and one season, his most recent, with the Hokkaido Nippon Ham Fighters. His statistics were solid across the board, and he spent time as both a starter and reliever. Okajima was certainly a well-respected pitcher, but lacked the movie star status of his counterpart Matsuzaka.

In comparison to the massive contracts signed by Matsuzaka, Lugo, and Drew, Okajima's payment was chump change. That disparity considered, Okajima proved to be Theo's greatest investment during the 2007 season. However, the season didn't start as well as Okajima would have liked it to.

On Opening Day, with the Sox already trailing 5-1, Francona made a move to the bullpen. The opposing Royals had smacked Schilling around, touching him up for five earned runs in just four innings, and left-hander Javier Lopez replaced Schilling in the fifth. After Lopez's scoreless inning of work, Okajima trotted out of the bully. In a true "welcome to the big leagues" moment, Kansas City's catcher John Buck greeted Hideki rudely.

Okajima went into his unorthodox wind-up and let go of a high-80's fastball. Buck, an unusually tall catcher at 6-foot-3, 210 pounds, was looking for a heater to jump on early in the count. The burly backstop unloaded on Okajima's fastball, depositing the baseball over the center field fence for a no-doubter of a home run.

One batter, one hit surrendered, one earned run—nice

way to start a major league career. Watching the majestic shot sail over the wall, Red Sox fans were thinking, "Well, at least he helped us get Dice-K."

But Okajima's failure was only momentary; he would very quickly make a name for himself. He remained in the game after the Buck home run, and recorded five outs without allowing a run. From there, he was off and running. Okajima proceeded to become one of Boston's most valuable players in 2007, finishing sixth in the American League Rookie of the Year voting while being selected to his first All-Star Game. Okajima's incredible success came as a huge surprise to most; executives around the league were shaking their heads, wondering, "Why didn't we get that guy?"

Did Theo foresee Okajima's dominance, or did he get lucky? The money the Sox spent on Hideki suggested that they weren't that high on him, or at the very least, they weren't expecting him to be an All-Star caliber reliever. However, a more likely explanation than luck is that Theo knew he was getting a steal in Okajima at about $1.25 million per season. He had an excellent international scouting department at his disposal, and Shipley and others noticed something about Okajima that could make him very effective in the big leagues: his delivery.

Okajima delivered the ball directly over the top, giving him the ability to "pitch downhill" (a favorite phrase of major league scouts). Pitching downhill requires a pitcher to sit on his back leg, better known as the "drive leg," for as long as possible, which promotes a north-south style, as opposed to east-west. A "north-south" pitcher is one who features a straight, four-seam fastball, and off-speed pitches that move downward, not across. Sliders and cutters move horizontally, curveballs and splitters drop down—Okajima, fitting the mold, threw a curve and two different types of splitters, according to Shipley.

And there was something else about Okajima, something very strange. Okajima would wind up, start toward the plate, get to the point of release... and look down. Believe it or not, he would turn his head slightly to the right and face the ground. There's never been a blind pitcher in the history of the major leagues, but Okajima essentially blinds himself when he lets go of the ball. He's not in the best position to field a line drive back to the mound, to say the least.

Bizarre, unique, dangerous, but effective; Theo and his scouting department had correctly identified Okajima's unorthodoxy as a potential strength in the bigs. Not to mention the fact that he's a lefty—lefties are always at a premium.

So Theo hit the jackpot with Okajima, but how would the rest of his investments fare in 2007?

Not so well in the regular season. Dice-K was solid but miles away from spectacular. His 15 victories were encouraging, but he also lost 12 games while putting up an alarmingly high 4.40 ERA. A 4.40 can be considered OK for an American League pitcher, but for over $100 million, it's safe to say that Theo was looking for better than OK (understatement of the century). Dice-K did manage to crack the 200-strikeout barrier, with 201 but gave up 25 bombs. Fenway Park was not yet a friend of Matsuzaka's.

Lugo and Drew were disasters. The speedy shortstop hit .237 with an embarrassingly low .294 on-base percentage. Considering Theo's love for OBP, Lugo definitely caused him some sleepless nights. Perhaps Theo took the tissue money out of Julio's contract.

In addition, Lugo's inability to reach base took him out of the equation for the leadoff spot, but we'll get to that later.

Drew had a decent season by Theo's standards (.373 OBP, .423 slugging), but to Red Sox Nation, their new right fielder was a bust. He hit just .270 with 11 homers and 64 RBI. Relatively speaking, it was easily the least productive season of Drew's career. He surprisingly managed to stay healthy, playing in 140 games, but failed miserably in his attempt to solidify the No. 5 spot behind Ortiz and Manny. Drew improved Boston's outfield defense, but that wasn't enough to quiet the complaints of the Red Sock faithful.

During Red Sox broadcasts on NESN (the New England Sports Network), television cameras would find Theo sweating out Drew's at bats. On the rare occasions that he came through, Theo would celebrate with a fist pump or another unusually candid celebration. It was clear that his membership in the J.D. Drew Fan Club would not be expiring any time soon.

On his metaphorical regular season stat sheet, Theo was 1-for-4. He ripped an extra-base hit with Okajima, but Lugo and Drew were easy outs. He battled up there with Matsuzaka, but he too had to be considered an out. It was far from an all-star off-season for Theo; his hypothetical .250 batting average was Shipley-esque.

Despite the underwhelming performances of Lugo, Drew, and Matsuzaka, Theo's boys returned to the playoffs after a year off in 2006. The big-name acquisitions of the '05-06 off-season, Josh Beckett and Mike Lowell, picked up the slack in '07. Beckett was beastly, finishing second to Cleveland's C.C. Sabathia in the AL Cy Young Award voting, with 20 wins and a 3.27 ERA. Sox management hoped Beckett would make adjustments for Fenway Park in '07, and he did. He found his vicious curveball and threw it with greater consistency.

Lowell turned out to be one of the best stories of the season. Two years removed from a trade in which he was a throw-in, he stuck it to his critics by having the most sensational all-around season of his big league career. Lowell supplanted Drew as Boston's No. 5 batter, hitting .324 with 21 dingers and 120 RBI. His .378 OBP and .501 slugging percentage weren't too shabby, either. Lowell's statistics and nearly flawless defense earned him a well-deserved fifth-place finish in the American League MVP race.

The '07 additions to the Red Sox struggled collectively,

but the newbie class of '06 tore it up. Theo didn't officially have a hand in the trade with the Marlins (the credit had to go to Lucchino, Lajoie, and Shipley at the time), but had to breathe a sigh of relief watching Beckett and Lowell come alive in their second season with his club.

The former Fish weren't the only duo to impress in 2007, a pair of the Epstein regime's draft picks—second baseman Dustin Pedroia and outfielder Jacoby Ellsbury—proved invaluable to Boston's postseason success. Pedroia was a second-round pick of Theo's in '04, and Ellsbury was a first-round selection in '05. Both players had a knack for getting on base, and the tandem would share time at the leadoff spot throughout the playoffs. The Sox's other options for the No. 1 spot, Lugo and Coco Crisp, produced next to nothing offensively.

Theo's strong drafting allowed him to cover his own back. Even better, Pedroia and Ellsbury looked like long-term solutions at second base and in center field.

However, Theo was still a little uneasy about his team, particularly its bullpen. If his starting pitchers could get the ball to Okajima in the eighth inning, it was lights out. The league couldn't figure out the rookie left-hander, and the virtually automatic Papelbon followed him in the ninth. But of course, starters don't throw seven innings every night anymore, so it was the men in the middle that concerned Theo. Timlin was 41 years old and American League hitters seemed to be all over his fastball, and flame-thrower Manny Delcarmen's lack of experience made him a question mark in high-pressure situations. The media raved about Okajima and Papelbon, but grumbled about the rest of Theo's relief core. The trade deadline approached, and Theo wasn't about to let it pass quietly.

In a seven-player deal involving both the Texas Rangers and Atlanta Braves, Theo acquired right-handed closer Eric Gagné of the Rangers. Gagné, the goggled-geared reliever (remember that Theo used to wear goggles when he played sports, so maybe that's why he liked Gagné) known for his look and a devastating arsenal of pitches, was once the most dominant closer in the game. Incredibly, and almost inexplicably, as a member of the Dodgers he saved 84 consecutive games in a streak that began in late August of 2002 and ended on July 5, 2004. Gagné outdid the previous major league record for consecutive saves, that of Tom "Flash" Gordon's (a former player of the Red Sox), by 30.

Yet three seasons later, Gagné was hardly the same pitcher. The burly hurler underwent Tommy John surgery in '05, and battled a severe back injury in '06. During that time he lost his air of invincibility, and was no longer considered one of baseball's elite closers. In '07 the Rangers gave Gagné a shot at the back of their bullpen, and it paid off. In a half-season renaissance, Gagné put up a tidy 2.16 ERA and recorded 16 saves with Texas. Those numbers were enough to convince Theo of his value, but he wasn't always a "Gagné guy."

In "The Mitchell Report," the famous 409-page document chronicling the possible users and abusers of performance-enhancing drugs in Major League Baseball, there's a segment about Theo's dealings with Gagné. This was not a document that Theo wanted his name in. Here's the excerpt:

> When the Boston Red Sox were considering acquiring Gagné, a Red Sox official made specific inquiries about Gagné's possible use of steroids. In a November 1, 2006 e-mail to a Red Sox scout, general manager Theo Epstein asked, "Have you done any digging on Gagné? I know the Dodgers think he was a steroid guy. Maybe so. What did you hear on his medical?" (p 219)

Theo's scout, Mark Delpiano, told him that Gagné was in fact a "steroid guy." He said that he questioned Gagné's commitment to staying healthy and in shape, and Theo knew a red flag when he saw one. He passed on Gagné that off-season, but couldn't overlook his short-lived success in Texas. Gagné's numbers looked good to Theo, and the league was buzzing about his apparent return to form. Despite his struggles in the previous two years, Gagné remained a big-name player. His addition would put smiles to the faces of the Red Sox faithful, and muzzles on the mouths of media members ready to attack Theo for staying put at the deadline.

Once again, Theo fell victim to the trade deadline

frenzy. Thirty-three innings of solid work wasn't enough of an indication of Gagné's post-Tommy John ability. In '05 and '06 Gagné appeared in just 16 games—combined. Like his deadline move for right-handed reliever Todd Jones in '03, the Gagné trade also constituted a miserable failure. Somehow, Gagné was even worse than Jones was for the Red Sox. The smiles on the faces of the Fenway fans were turned upside down by Gagné's embarrassingly high 6.75 ERA. Add him to the "bust" pile.

The Red Sox dealt with their fair share of question marks and disappointments during the regular season, but to the delight of Red Sox Nation, Theo's gang pulled it all together in the playoffs. Boston cruised past the Los Angeles Angels of Anaheim in the AL Division series, sweeping them into the off-season without breaking a sweat. Beckett headlined game 1 with a complete-game, four-hit shutout that included eight eye-popping strike-outs. Manny Ramirez had a clutch three-run homer off "K-Rod" (Angels closer Francisco Rodriguez) in the ninth inning of game 2, and the Sox pounded out 10 hits and nine runs in game 3 to beat the Angels by eight.

For Boston, the series was reminiscent of the 2005 ALDS against the White Sox, only this time they were on the other end of the sweep.

In the American League Championship Series, the Red Sox rallied dramatically from a 3-1 deficit against the Cleveland Indians, showing the same resiliency as the 2004 World Series team. Theo's roster moves were often statistically based, but he also knew how to spot players with the heart and guts necessary to produce when the tension reaches its highest point. One of the players that proved his instincts correct was J.D. Drew.

Drew continued his Division Series slump that began with the Braves in 2004, hitting .182 with no homers against the Angels. But the slump wouldn't continue for long—Drew came up with the biggest hit of his career in the ALCS.

With the Sox trailing 3-2 in the series, Drew stepped to the plate in the bottom of the first with the bases loaded and two outs. Staring down at him from the hill was Fausto Carmona, a fiery young right-hander whom MLB analysts had dubbed a "turbo-sinkerballer" in recent months. Sinkerballers typically throw in the 88-to-92 mph range; Fausto earned the "turbo" distinction by running his sinker up there as quickly as 97 mph. Carmona dazzled many throughout his breakout regular season, and the 23-year-old had pitched very well in the preceding series against the Yankees.

It was a big situation for Drew, and a difficult match-up. Theo crept up to the edge of his seat.

With the Fenway faithful on their feet, Drew got himself a pitch to drive. Like all sinkerballers, Carmona was at his best with the ball down in the zone. This one came in around the belt, and Drew put a charge into it. The shot sailed into center field, the deepest part of the park, and Indians' centerfielder Grady Sizemore looked as if he might have a beat on it. Sizemore drifted back onto the warning track, further back toward the wall, and looked up…

It was gone.

Drew trotted around the bases, stoic as ever, as Fenway's foundation rocked. Sox fans everywhere mobbed each other. Up in his overlooking front office box, Theo rejoiced with a double fist pump. His beloved Drew had finally come through.

Drew's first-inning grand slam proved to be the game-winning hit, as the Indians mustered up only two runs against the trio of Schilling, Javier Lopez, and Eric Gagné. The Sox won game 6 by a final score of 12-2, and buried the Indians with an impressive 11-2 victory in the decisive game 7.

It was on to the World Series, where the Sox would meet the youthful, exciting, and streaking Colorado Rockies. Incredibly, the Rocks had won 21 of their previous 22 games, including a three-game sweep of the Phillies in the NLDS, and a four-game sweep of the Arizona Diamondbacks in the NLCS. The D'backs were another young, upstart team, but they proved to be no match for the rightfully confident Rockies.

Colorado was undefeated to that point in the '07 playoffs, but the Sox didn't appear to be too concerned. Theo and company were on what poker players would call a "free roll," that is, they were in a no-lose situation after fighting off elimination on three separate occasions against the Indians. The Sox had little fear of losing after dancing closely with postseason doom. They had been to the edge and back, so to speak.

There were eight Red Sox holdovers from the '04 championship team, accounting for a little less than 1/3 of the 2007 World Series roster. They were: Ramirez, Ortiz, Schilling, Varitek, Wakefield, Youkilis, Timlin, and Doug Mirabelli. Of the eight, only three—Ortiz, Schilling, and Timlin—were "Theo guys" (players he originally drafted, signed, or traded for).

Things had changed a little from the first time around. Ramirez, Ortiz, Schilling, Varitek, and Timlin would be used in virtually the same capacity, but Wakefield was forced off the '07 World Series roster with severe right shoulder inflammation. The knuckleballer was replaced by Kyle Snyder, a right-handed long man with the durability to start in the case of an emergency. Youkilis was a reserve in 2004, the last man added to the World Series roster, but this time he was a starter and essential offensive contributor. Mirabelli would again play second fiddle to Varitek, but wasn't a true holdover—the veteran signal caller spent the '06 season with the San Diego Padres. Theo was forced to bring Mirabelli back in '07 because younger back up Josh Bard had difficulty receiving Wakefield's knuckler.

Nevertheless, the Sox had a clear experience advantage over the Rockies. Like the wise, old mentor schooling the young protégé, Boston proceeded to teach Colorado a

World Series lesson that was sure to cause serious growing pains.

Not only did Theo's well-balanced roster put an end to the Rockies' 11-game winning streak in game 1, but it continued from there with three consecutive victories en route to Boston's second World Series sweep in four years. Theo's men proved they could win in any fashion, blowing out the Rocks in games 1 and 3, and clipping them with one-run victories in games 2 and 4.

"We earned it," Theo said after his boys closed the lid on the Rockies. "[Over the past few years] things have changed around here, we have guys who play their best baseball at the most important time of the year. There's a lot of heart and soul on this club; great mix of veterans, and young players, and a great manager."

Theo's free agent signings who underachieved during the regular season, Matsuzaka and Lugo, both came through in the postseason. Lugo made one beautiful defensive play after another, and Dice-K posted a flawless 3-0 record in four playoff starts. Matsuzaka even added a World Series victory to his impressive professional baseball resume, going 5 1/3 and surrendering just three hits in game 3.

Theo's draftees—Papelbon, Pedroia, and Ellsbury—shined on the big stage. Papelbon burned threw 4 1/3 innings without allowing a run, and picked up three saves in the process. Ellsbury hit an off-the-charts .438, while scoring four runs and driving in three. Pedroia tied for second on the team with four RBI in the series.

Quite simply, it all came together. The draft picks, the signings, the trade returns—in every way possible, Theo had painted a masterpiece.

Five years on the job, two World Series titles. Could life get any better for Theo Epstein?

Beyond the Game: Theo's Personal Life

In January of 2007, Theo Epstein broke the hearts of many young women in Boston when he tied the knot with his 28-year-old fiancée, Marie Whitney. Surprisingly enough, Theo and Marie were married in New York. Theo returned to his city of origin in order to protect the couple's privacy, and the two wedded rather quietly.

Even more surprising was where they decided to make their union official.

Theo and Marie became Mr. and Mrs. Epstein on Coney Island... at a Nathan's hot dog stand. They tried to hide their unusual arrangements from the world, but in an e-mail, Theo's father Leslie spilled the beans about the wacky wedding...

Just kidding. But in late January of '07, that's what *Sports Illustrated* and the *Boston Globe* reported. Two of the better-respected publications in America were duped by Theo's dad, the practical-joking professor from Boston University. Reporters had been hounding the Epstein family for weeks, trying to get inside information about the ceremony, so Leslie thought it would be funny to steer them in the wrong direction. The real comedic value, he felt, was in the fact that Theo's middle name was "Nathan." Theo Nathan getting married at Nathan's—Leslie got a kick out of the idea.

So *The Globe* had to bite its tongue, and print an update the following day. It read:

> Correction: A story in yesterday's Sports section quoted an e-mail by Theo Epstein's father, Leslie, as saying the Red Sox general manager and his fiancee, Marie Whitney, had gotten married at Nathan's hot dog stand at Coney Island, N.Y. Leslie Epstein said yesterday he had been joking about where the wedding took place. Details of the ceremony have remained secret at the request of Theo Epstein.

Score one for the Epsteins. Dan Shaughnessy had taken shots at Theo in *The Globe* before, so it didn't hurt to even things up a little. *Sports Illustrated* had the story posted on their website, and once it was found to be loaded with misinformation, they killed the link. Today, members of the *SI* staff pretend as if the story never existed.

As far as serious information went, Leslie provided little to the two outlets.

"We're very happy for them, of course, but we can't say much more," he said. "I hope there's much happiness for them and for all Sox fans this season."

With the protective shield wrapped tightly around Theo's personal life, it was difficult for anyone to discover the reality of his wedding—if it didn't take place at Nathan's, then where?

Details of the proposal had been exposed—in May of '06, Theo popped the question at Davio's restaurant in the Back Bay area—but the wedding was being handled like Area 51 or a C.I.A. operation. Reporters began to question what was more important to Theo, protecting his family's privacy or throwing the media for a loop and laughing about it afterward. Even the proposal was quiet.

"They were just like any other couple out for dinner," said waiter Robert Mahon at the time. "She ordered for both of them. There was no champagne toast; I don't think she even drank! He had a vodka cocktail and that was it. When we read about the engagement in the papers, we were all a little surprised."

The engagement was quiet, the wedding a mystery, but at least there were a few leaks about the bachelor party.

Woooo, party! Theo goin' wild!

Sadly, it wasn't that interesting. Theo played it cool on one of the final evenings of his single life. While his friends chanted and yelled, "Theo! Theo!" the man of the hour was off in the corner, on his cell phone. Instead of swinging from a chandelier or taking twelve consecutive shots at the bar, according to *Boston Magazine,* Theo was checking in with Marie. "Hi, my little Pookie bear." Or something like that.

Finally, after some serious sleuth work, one of Boston's radio stations was able to piece the whole shebang together. The WFNX-FM radio station, 101.7 on the dial, reported that Theo and Marie were married on a yacht toward the beginning of January. ESPN seconded the report on their website.

The commander-in-chief of the yacht was none other than John W. Henry, the principal owner of the Boston Red Sox. Henry is a huge fan of Theo's and wanted to ensure an elegant but private celebration for his GM and bride. Henry was distraught over Theo's decision to leave after the '05 season, and in letting baseball's most successful young executive get away, he questioned his ability to run a Major League Baseball team. Ever since, Henry had been looking for a way to thank Theo for returning, and lending his yacht seemed like a good start. It was a wonderful gesture on Henry's part, both personally and professionally. Classy decisions like that are what get him mentioned among the best owners in all of sports.

With that, Theo and Marie were officially hitched. Before beginning her volunteer work, Marie was a graduate student at Harvard focusing on health care policies.

Harvard? Theo graduated from Yale. What was he thinking?

Perhaps Theo had forgotten about the heated Harvard-Yale rivalry. Nah, that wasn't possible. The answer was simple: he was more than willing to make an exception for Marie. The days of, "Is It Time for Carm to Go?" were long behind him. Marie had a big smile and an even bigger heart, and Theo wasn't about to let her Harvard history get in their way.

According to *The Globe*, the happy couple followed up their lovely wedding with a week overseas.

Marie has since been volunteering with Horizons for Hopeless Children (HHC), a group that nurtures homeless children and addresses their needs. HHC connects children who were formerly in shelters to families in the Greater Boston area. Their mission statement reflects an organization that more people should be aware of:

> We help children learn how to play, to share, to read, and to enjoy exploring their worlds. We help parents learn how to be nurturing and involved in the growth and development of their children, and help them learn and grow through job training, GED and college courses. We help to stabilize families so that they can weather any crisis, and thus help to break the cycle of homelessness that too often occurs.

There's no question that Marie donates her time to a worthy cause. HHC has ties to cities and towns throughout Massachusetts, including Dorchester, Holyoke, Jamaica Plain, Lawrence, New Bedford, Roxbury, and Worcester.

On December 12, 2007, things changed drastically in the young marriage of Theo and Marie Epstein. No, it wasn't a domestic violence case or accusations of adultery—get your mind out of the gutter—it was the debut of their newest family member, the second coming of "The Wonder Boy," son, Jack. Theo and Marie had nothing to say to the media after the birth; a Red Sox's spokesman threw the only bone.

"Everybody is doing fine," said John Blake, now the club's vice president of Media Relations. "The family would appreciate some privacy."

When it comes to his family, such a response is typical from Theo. He's been described in publications as both "fiercely private about his personal life," and "a man with a serious commitment to privacy." *Boston Magazine* wrote, "Even his coworkers in the Sox front office don't know much about Epstein's private life."

As for Jack, he was born at 10:35 a.m. in a Boston hospital, weighing in at 7 pounds, 14 ounces. At 20.5 inches tall, Jack signified changes much larger than his stature. Theo and Marie would have to step things up, and move into a home with a little more real estate.

Beat reporters Carol Beggy and Mark Shanahan said that the couple used to live in a condo on St. Botolph Street in Boston. The condo had three bedrooms and "two-and-a-half" bathrooms, whatever that means. In lieu of "The Wonder Baby's" arrival, the Epsteins moved into a new home. They didn't mind saying goodbye to St. Botolph Street, the street where Theo's car was vandalized. They weren't upset about leaving the condo, a building that had obscenities spray-painted along its side. Along with little Jack, the Epsteins set up shop in the upscale village of Chestnut Hill, Massachusetts. They were happy to have some acquaintances in the area: the Francona and Lucchino families. As if Theo didn't see enough of Terry and Larry at the ballpark.

The Epsteins new home had its perks: five bedrooms and a near perfect location. It was a short distance from the Brookline apartment where Theo grew up. Just like the old days, he wouldn't have to travel far to get to Fenway. In a way, Theo's life had come full circle—an unusual experience for a 33-year-old. Nonetheless, he embraced the newest chapter in his story.

In addition to family endeavors, Theo's had other things cookin' in his life away from baseball. He has a relatively steady hobby: playing the guitar. Theo began strumming during his days in San Diego, and a few years back, his mother, Ilene, bought him a brand-new guitar for his birthday. How she decided on the type of guitar is quite a story.

Ilene assumed that Theo would love her present no matter what; regardless, she wanted to get him the best possible model. The problem was neither Leslie, Paul nor Sandy knew much about the top guitars on the market, so

Ilene had to tap into her son's celebrity status, something Theo rarely ever does. Ilene decided that calling the local guitar shop just wasn't going to cut it… it was time for her to go big or go home. So she picked up the phone and put in a call to Eddie Vedder's manager.

Yup, *the* Eddie Vedder. For a refresher, Vedder is the lead singer of Pearl Jam, one of Theo's favorite rock groups, a band that has produced gold, platinum, and multi-platinum records. Ilene should have asked Tiger Woods to recommend a set of golf clubs while she was at it.

After some discussion and deliberation, she settled on a Rickenbacker. It was a conservative but classy choice. Rickenbacker produced the very first electric guitars back in 1932, and the company has enjoyed booming business ever since. Ilene followed in Theo's general managerial footsteps, making a can't-miss decision.

As expected, Theo loved his mother's gift. He immediately went to work sharpening his skills and getting a feel for his new guitar, and it wasn't long before he was on stage playing it in front of a crowd. He was not a performance rookie; in fact, Theo tore down the house at Peter Gammons' 2003 Hot Stove, Cool Music charity event— the same event where his gorilla suit was auctioned off a couple years later. With his band, Trauser, Theo played a few covers. Of note, one of the covers was of a Pearl Jam song.

But those were Theo's pre-Rickenbacker days. He

eventually introduced his pretty, new guitar to the world at the 2006 Hot Stove, Cool Music concert. Theo jammed with Buffalo Tom, an alternative rock band from Boston that debuted in the early '80s and picked up steam with the public in the '90s. Buffalo Tom had a strong following at the charity event, and their fans were shocked and amazed to see Theo keeping up with their favorite musicians. Theo was a smash hit, as was Ilene's birthday present.

"They say all baseball players want to be rock stars and vice versa, which I find to be a little bit true," Theo said.

He went on to perform again at the 2007 and 2008 shows. Along the way, Theo played a few side sessions with his new friend, Vedder. Ilene's initial call opened the door to a friendship for tabloids to drool over. The two apparently have good musical chemistry, and Pearl Jam loves the Red Sox.

Back at home Theo continues to handle things internally. Even with the names of his wife and child out there in the open, he doesn't say much about them publicly or privately. Most of his colleagues and coworkers know very little about Marie, and that's the way Theo likes it. In the past Theo and Marie have been spotted shopping, eating out and even skiing, but understandably, the couple now devotes the overwhelming majority of their time to their son.

Theo and his son, Jack

When he's not playing his guitar or spending time with his family, Theo keeps up on his politics. His 2008 presidential election cards have been revealed. Along with a contingency of big names from a number of different realms, including Ben Affleck, Jennifer Aniston, Tyra Banks, Warren Buffett, Danny DeVito, Michael Douglas, Jamie Foxx, Morgan Freeman, Bill Gates, John Grisham, Tom Hanks, Hugh Hefner, Dustin Hoffman, Samuel L. Jackson, Stephon Marbury, Dave Matthews, Chris Rock, Emmitt Smith, Will Smith, Steven Spielberg, Ben Stiller, and Oprah Winfrey (to name some), Theo was a registered member of "Obama for America," the official presidential campaign for the U.S. senator from Illinois. In voting Democratic, Theo appears to have followed his father's lead.

Leslie, one of the truest of all Yankee haters, once said that rooting for the Bronx Bombers was "like voting Republican."

Like father, like son. Theo has certainly inherited some of his father's personality and ideology. In more than just politics—in life—Theo can only hope that little Jack will follow in *his* footsteps.

Will another intelligent, well-spoken, upstanding Epstein hold the keys to the Red Sox in the future?

Just like the rest of us, Theo will have to wait and see.

Is Theo as Good as His Results?

"**T**heo Epstein stinks. Isn't that pretty much the consensus?"

That's what Bill Burt, Massachusetts sports columnist
and radio personality, wrote in *The Eagle-Tribune* prior to
the 2007 American League Championship Series. Burt
questioned and attacked some of Theo's roster moves, but
also praised the Red Sox's GM for others. The point of the
article wasn't to bash Theo, but to bring the town's rumblings to the forefront…

Beantown was souring on its golden boy. The "consensus" was this: Theo Epstein's success was *not* a product
of his beautiful mind, Yale education, background with
the Orioles and Padres, or unique style of evaluating and
assessing players; his success was a product of the endless
funding provided by Red Sox principal owner John Henry
and chairman Tom Werner.

Is there truth to that notion?

You can decide that for yourself. Here are the best

and worse general managerial decisions of Theo's six-year reign:

THE WORST!

> **WORST MOVE** *Honorable Mention*:
> **Signing SS Edgar Renteria to a four-year deal.**

This is one of the most talked about failures of Theo's career, but simply put, it's not as bad as some of his others. Theo signed Renteria prior to the 2005 season, and although he was coming off a bit of a down year in '04, he was only 29 years old. Renteria was a key offensive player for the 1997 World Series champion Florida Marlins, and added to his big-game experience during his six-year run with the St. Louis Cardinals. In sports it's rightfully said that it's "always more difficult to repeat," so Theo looked to improve his defending champion roster wherever possible. Orlando Cabrera performed well for the Sox following the Nomar Garciaparra trade, but few baseball insiders ranked him above Renteria heading into the '05 season.

Renteria hit over .300 in '02 and '03, and remained very solid at .287 in 2004. Most considered him one of the top five offensive shortstops in the game, and Theo's assumption was that the Green Monster would make him even more productive. It was a fair assumption, because Renteria had stroked 36 or more doubles in each of the previous three seasons. As a strong gap hitter, he could only be expected to improve in Boston.

Unfortunately for Theo and the rest of the Red Sox organization, the 2005 season turned out to be one of the worst—if not *the* worst—of Renteria's 10-year career. Boston's shortstop hit just .276 with eight home runs, after finishing with double-digit homers every year since 1999. In addition to poor production, Renteria struggled mightily with his glove, leading the majors in errors, with 30. He poured gasoline on the fire by blaming his struggles on poor infield conditions at Fenway Park.

Red Sox Nation called for Renteria's head, and they got their wish: 2005 would prove to be the only year Renteria spent in a Red Sox uniform. In December, in Theo's absence, Bill Lajoie and Craig Shipley traded Renteria to the Atlanta Braves for a highly touted third base prospect, a big right-handed hitter named Andy Marte.

Marte eventually became the key piece to move from Boston to Cleveland in the Coco Crisp trade. The deal for Crisp is another that Theo is attacked for, but the Sox didn't lose much in the exchange. Marte, by all intents and purposes, has been a bust, while Crisp at the very least provides above-average defense in centerfield. Coco hasn't hit as well as Theo or Red Sox fans would like him too, but he always plays hard and occasionally saves runs with his glove.

Returning to Renteria, yes, he failed to produce for Theo, but to say the signing was illogical would be incorrect. Some analysts suggested that Renteria was on the downside of his career when Theo picked him up, but the veteran shortstop went on to a hit a career-high .332 for the Braves in 2007. Often it's said that some players "can't play in New York"—well, Renteria just couldn't cut it in Boston.

WORST MOVE # 5
Trading for RP Eric Gagné.

Prior to the 2007 season, when scout Mark Delpiano questioned Gagné's work ethic and the durability of his arm, Theo decided to pass on the once dominant closer. Theo trusted his scouts and the rest of his player evaluation team, so he allowed Gagné to slip away and sign with the Texas Rangers during the off-season. But Gagné got off to a flying start in '07, and Texas' failures made him available around the trade deadline.

Theo is astutely aware of ballpark effects, and the Rangers' Ballpark in Arlington has been one of the best offensive yards in baseball history. Gagné's success—to the tune of a 2.16 ERA and 16 saves—was an aberration, and the possibility that he had returned to his old form had to be considered.

The best option would have been to evaluate Gagné's stuff. During his prime with the Los Angeles Dodgers,

Gagné's fastball exploded through the zone at 95 to 98 mph. With Texas, he was lucky to scratch 95 with his absolute best heater. Gagné was more consistently in the 91-to-94 range, and his movement was straight across as opposed to sinking across *and* down.

Gagné's change-up, a pitch that once rivaled Mariano Rivera's cutter as the most effective in the world, was still good. However, it was no longer a lights-out weapon because it had become easier for hitters to catch up to Gagné's fastball. With the ability to react late to his fastball, batters could guess change-up a little more and put good wood on it with greater regularity.

Gagné's third pitch, a heavy overhand curveball, had nearly fallen out of his arsenal. The big cranker often places stress upon a pitcher's elbow and shoulder, and with a history of arm trouble, Gagné wasn't about to open the door to another surgery. He mixed in a curve occasionally, but primarily threw fastballs and change-ups.

Scouts and pitching coaches often say that a relief pitcher can be successful with a pair of "plus" pitches. A "plus" pitch is a strong pitch, one that is clearly better than average. But in his better days Gagné had three plus pitches, and that's what made him unique and virtually unhittable.

By the time Theo was ready to trade for him, Gagné was down to one plus pitch: his "fast-change." No, that's not an actual pitch, but neither his fastball nor change could still be considered exceptional. Counting both pitches as halves and then adding them together, Gagné possessed equal value to a pitcher with a single plus pitch.

And yet, Theo decided to trust the numbers. Gagné was fairly close to a strikeout per inning, which meant he was getting his share of swings and misses and/or locating well. Whatever it was, Gagné was getting the job done, and Theo wanted to improve his bullpen. Despite the deteriorated stuff, Theo pulled the trigger and acquired Gagné in a seven-player deal involving three teams. He sent youngsters Kason Gabbard, David Murphy, and Engel Beltre packing.

Initially, Red Sox Nation was ecstatic. They marveled at the possibilities with Gagné, Hideki Okajima, and Jonathan Papelbon at the back of their bullpen. But the trio failed to meet expectations, and it was all Gagné's fault. The newest Red Sox player got beat up like a piñata at Fenway. Lollipops and "sucking" candies were flying around all over the stadium.

Perhaps there was another factor for Theo to consider: the weather. Gagné was able to keep his shoulder and arm loose in Texas' warm, sometimes steamy weather; but September in Boston got a little chilly. Gagné had been a warm-weather pitcher throughout his career—having spent parts of eight seasons with the Dodgers—and the New England cold couldn't possibly favor his sensitive arm. At Fenway Gagné would enter games with a little stiffness, sometimes throwing his fastball as slowly as 90 mph.

Ninety miles per hour is by no means slow—the average person would be lucky to foul tip a pitch at that speed—but in the big leagues, 90 is right around the norm. Gagné used to be a fearless, intimidating force, but it's hard to be intimidating when you're throwing as hard as a decent high school prospect. The American League hitters, particularly those in the AL East, feasted on Gagné. Theo's newest big-name acquisition pitched to a minor-league worthy 6.75 ERA. Nothing positive came of the deal.

Gabbard, a left-handed starting pitcher, was 4-0 for the Red Sox at the time of the trade. Gabbard never possessed impressive stuff, but had decent control and a knack for picking up victories; critics wondered why Theo was so willing to part with a young lefty.

Murphy, an outfielder with the versatility to play left, right, and center, broke out with the Rangers this season. He hit .275 with 15 homers and 74 RBI in 108 games as a starter for Texas, before going down with an unfortunate season-ending injury. A nice lefty bat, Murphy would have been a perfect fourth or fifth outfielder for the Red Sox this year.

Murphy looks like more of a long-term keeper right now, but neither he nor Gabbard was worth Gagné. The trade was irrational, and showed a little desperation on Theo's part. The only reasons it's not higher up on the list are (1) because he didn't make a long-term commitment to Gagné, and (2) the Red Sox still managed to win the World Series.

WORST MOVE # 4
Re-signing Byung-Hyun Kim to a two-year, $10 million contract to be a starting pitcher.

Bad. Bad. Bad. It was an inking that made no sense at the time, and makes even less sense in hindsight. At the time, it was difficult to find a baseball mind that felt Kim was worth $5 million a year as a starting pitcher. In seven starts with Arizona in 2003, Kim did fine, posting a 3.56 ERA. But the sidewinder hadn't shown the ability to win, going just 1-5 before being traded to the Sox.

Though Kim had pitched the beginning of games overseas, his arm angle made it nearly impossible to project him as a successful major league starter. He was tough on righties, but after his first couple of years with Arizona, lefties caught on to his sinker away. If Kim was worth anywhere near $5 million a season, it was as a reliever. The Yankees rocked his world in 2001, but B.K. bounced back nicely as a bullpen guy in both '02 and '03.

Theo had other rotation options in '04. At the top, he boasted an exceptional one through four in Pedro Martinez, Curt Schilling, Derek Lowe, and Tim Wakefield. Pedro and Schilling represented the premier 1-2 punch in the bigs, and Lowe and Wakefield were considered among the best in their respective rotation slots. Considering the strength of his top four, there was little need for Theo to break the bank on a No. 5 starter. A pitcher who could throw strikes and keep his team in the game every fifth day would have sufficed.

Theo's younger options were Bronson Arroyo, Lenny DiNardo, and longshot Jonathan Papelbon. Arroyo, a deceptive right-hander, had been a well-regarded prospect in the Pirates' organization a few years earlier. His fastball wasn't overpowering, but he featured a Frisbee slider that was undoubtedly a plus. In 17.3 innings of work for Boston in '03, Arroyo pitched to a promising 2.08 ERA. He wasn't too experienced, but was much cheaper than Kim, and worth a shot.

Arroyo eventually filled the five slot for the Red Sox, but by that time, it was too late. Theo had already re-signed Kim and the little man was nursing the emotional bruises of falling flat on his face.

If Theo was unsure about Arroyo, DiNardo was a little more polished. He too was young, but the tall left-hander was a former high draft pick of the New York Mets. Like Arroyo he wasn't a flamethrower, but DiNardo was a crafty lefty in the mold of the aforementioned Gabbard. He could certainly pick up some victories with help from Boston's powerful offense.

Papelbon wasn't a realistic option at the beginning of the 2004 season because he had just been selected in the '03 draft. But of the three youngsters, Papelbon had the best stuff. There was a small possibility that he could emerge as an option during the second half of the year.

Even if Theo wanted nothing to do with the younger

arms, righty reliever Ramiro Mendoza was a starter earlier in his career with the Yankees. Mendoza tanked in his first year as a member of Boston's relief core, so it wouldn't have hurt to try him out as a starter. Most teams are flexible with their fifth starters over the course of the long season, and it was unnecessary for Theo to drop $10 million on an unproven commodity. He went against his theory of building from the farm system, and instead overpaid like the rival Yankees would.

In three starts, Kim posted a bloated 6.23 ERA in 2004. Ugly. B.K. struggled with injuries and control and was eventually cut loose by the Sox.

Ten million dollars for three starts, and lousy ones at that—instead of bang for his buck, Theo got silence. Similarly to the Gagné move, this would have been higher up on the list of disasters... if the Red Sox had failed to win it all in 2004.

They didn't.

WORST MOVE # 3
The risky bullpen experiment in 2003.

It's clear that Theo was looking to make a splash in his first official year on the job, and maybe that's because of the experience he gained as "assistant GM" in '02. (Though we now know, he was basically the GM that season, too.) Sources inside baseball have said Theo's interchangeable parts bullpen "wasn't a bad idea," and that it "may have worked in the long run," and perhaps that's the case. But in the short term, it turned out to be a miserable laughingstock.

It wasn't a necessary ideological maneuver. Theo was looking to unleash some game-changing baseball philosophy upon the league, but ultimately his relievers became confused about their roles and performed significantly below their expected levels. Two months hadn't passed before Theo was basically forced into a move for—speak of the devil—Byung-Hyun Kim.

Bill James, senior advisor to Baseball Operations, said the committee would work if the relievers were of similar ability and value. With a group that ranged from crappy Steve Woodard to rock solid Mike Timlin (who became a keeper), Theo missed the mark. He probably could have re-signed closer Ugueth Urbina, who went on to save 32 games in 2003.

It was a brash experiment, and some might applaud Theo's aggressiveness, but it didn't pay off. If the interchangeable parts bullpen was such a great idea, don't you think Theo would have tried it again?

No need to bother when he has a guy like Jonathan Papelbon. That's what he needed back in '03, too.

WORST MOVE # 4

Signing SS Julio Lugo to a four-year deal worth $36 million.

Nine million a year for a player who had never hit over 15 homers, never driven in more than 75 runs, never hit over .285, never scored 100 runs, and never had an OBP above .365.

That's quite a few "nevers."

And yet there was Theo, throwing stacks of money at the rail-bodied shortstop from the Dominican Republic. Why? Probably because he could. There didn't seem to be any other possible explanation.

Lugo's a shortstop that's always had the "nice player" label stuck to his back, but has never been anything special. A good defensive player and a slightly better than average hitter, he seemed to be worth six to seven million per season, at the most. But Theo knew he had plenty of money in the bank, so he shelled out the extra cash to fill the Red Sox's vacancy at short. Theo wasn't planning to bring back Alex Gonzalez and didn't have a big-league ready shortstop in the minors, so the necessity was there. Again, the Lugo signing reflected a sense of desperation.

Lugo couldn't have been much worse in 2007, hitting a career-low .237 with an OBP below .300, the Mendoza line of on-base percentage. His regular season defense was a little shaky, but to his credit, he picked it up during the postseason. However, his weak bat evened out his performance in the playoffs.

As if Lugo's eight homers in '07 weren't cause enough for concern, he made Theo look even worse in '08. Not only did Lugo continue to show why he's considered injury-prone (missed 80 games), but he also hit just .268 with *one* homer in 261 at bats. Count 'em. One. One big one.

Lugo has battled an injury and if and when he does return, he probably won't be Terry Francona's starting shortstop. Rookie Jed Lowrie, a switch hitter, had 46 RBI in 260 at bats, to Lugo's 22 in 261. Lowrie gave the Red Sox better production and versatility with the lumber. In addition, he had 67 hits, 25 doubles, 35 walks, and a knack for using the Green Monster to his advantage—a great habit for a young player to have.

Lowrie's early success shouldn't come as a total surprise to Theo… he drafted the youngster as a supplemental first-round pick in the 2005 draft. That begs the question: Why would he need to sign a mediocre shortstop to a four-year deal worth $36 million if he had a first-round talent in the minor leagues?

For an executive who says he likes to build from his farm system, Theo didn't appear too confident in his scouts' evaluation of Lowrie. Lugo's contract is up after the 2010 season, which means Lowrie would have had to spend five seasons in the minors or on the big team's bench before he could get the opportunity to start.

Well, that was *if* Lugo performed up to par. He sure as hell hasn't.

Lugo's quadriceps injury caused him to miss about half of the '08 season, and he may not return to full strength in '09. This off-season Theo will be left with a $9 million shortstop with zero trade value. Two years left on his contract, no pop left in his bat, and a history of injuries— that's three strikes on Lugo's resume.

All aspects considered, Lowrie will probably be the Opening Day starter next year, making Lugo a $36 million bench player. Yikes.

San Diego Padres' general manager Kevin Towers pointed to this signing as one of the poorest of Theo's career as an executive. However, it isn't the absolute worst because the Sox managed to win the '07 World Series with Lugo as their shortstop.

WORST MOVE # 1

Signing SP Matt Clement to a three-year contract worth $25 million.

This one takes the cake. At no point in Matt Clement's seven-year career did his performance suggest that he was worth over $8 million per season. Prior to signing with the Red Sox, in his six seasons as a regular starting pitcher, Clement had a losing record four times. The two years he finished over .500, his records were 12-11 and 14-12. He joined the Sox with a 69-75 career record, and a 4.34 lifetime ERA. There was little reason for Theo to expect Clement to be an exceptional No. 2 or 3 starter, yet for the money he dished out, it seemed like that was exactly what he was expecting.

Clement had shown the ability to make hitters swing and miss, striking out 215 in '02, but often nullified his Ks with walks. Clement issued free passes to 85 or more batters for four consecutive seasons from 1999 to 2002. Inexplicably, he walked 125 batters in 2000. Talk about a red flag.

It was more like a bright neon pink flag.

Worst Move #1: Pitcher Matt Clement

But Clement's slight improvement in '03 and '04 appeared to be enough for Theo to trust him. The right-hander finished with less than 85 walks, but barely, with

79 in '03 and 77 in '04. Clement was a three-pitch pitcher who essentially limited himself to two. He had a fastball, slider, and change-up, but threw a fastball or change-up about 90 percent of the time. His slider was good, one of the most respected in the game, but the torque required to throw it was also cause for concern. Clement snapped off the slider, and it was only a matter of time before his arm felt the effects.

And it did. After posting a career-best 13-6 record in 2005—with plenty of help from Boston's potent lineup—Clement went on to appear in only 12 games in '06. Severe injuries to his labrum and rotator cuff derailed his Red Sox career. He hasn't appeared in a major league game since 2006, which of course, means that he failed to throw an inning for Theo in the third year of his unjustifiably lucrative contract. Clement was recently cut by the St. Louis Cardinals.

Not only did Theo overvalue Clement's ability, he failed to foresee the arm trouble that such a snap-slider could cause. Clement had been durable for a number of years preceding his tenure with the Red Sox, and health problems were inevitable.

Clement contributed in just one of his three seasons in Boston, and to make matters worse, he got annihilated in his single postseason start. The Chicago White Sox torched Clement in the playoffs.

During a lecture Theo gave alongside Yankees' GM Brian Cashman in New Jersey, at William Paterson University in January of this year, Theo pointed to the trade of right-handed pitcher Cla Meredith and catcher Josh Bard for catcher Doug Mirabelli as the worst move of his general managerial career.

It's really not even one of his worst six.

On May 2, 2006, Theo re-acquired Mirabelli after trading him to the Padres for Mark Loretta. The initial trade was a good move—Loretta was a solid offensive second baseman for Boston—but many of the Sox missed Mirabelli, especially knuckleballer Tim Wakefield.

Bard, a younger, less experienced backup catcher than Mirabelli, struggled mightily to receive Wakefield's devastating knuckler. His pitches would float, flutter, and fade away from Bard's glove, and it became increasingly more difficult for Wakefield to hold runners on base. When players started to complain to Theo about Bard's issues behind the dish, he felt he had to address their concerns. By bringing back Mirabelli, Theo lowered the number of pass balls during Wakefield starts, and made the veteran right-hander more comfortable when he let his unpredictable pitch go. The Red Sox's defense was more comfortable, as well.

But Theo regrets the deal because Bard and Meredith were much better long-term options for roster spots. Bard, a former third round pick of the Colorado Rockies, hit .338 for the Padres in 2006, and .285 in '07. A switch-hitting catcher with a little pop, Bard has more than few seasons left in him. Mirabelli, on the other hand, is finished.

Bard is solid, but Meredith was the bigger loss for

Theo. The side-arming righty was one of the best relievers in baseball in '06, pitching to a paper-thin 1.07 ERA in over 50 innings of work. Meredith's motion was deceptive, and he occasionally ran his sinker in there around 92 mph. His slurve was especially effective against right-handed hitters.

Still, there's no reason for Theo to cry over the spilt milk of this deal. Bard went all the way down to a .202 batting average this season, and National League hitters have figured out Meredith over the course of the past two years. His ERA increased from 1.07 to 3.50 in '07 and 4.09 in '08. A 3.50 ERA is OK, but 4.09 is bordering on mediocrity or worse. Meredith lost some velocity on his fastball and batters have figured out how to spot the ball quickly out of his hand.

Also, Meredith has played in San Diego's Petco Park, arguably the best pitchers' park in the majors. His strike-out per inning rate has been low, so there's reason to believe that he'd get touched up if Fenway Park was his home field. Really, Theo, this one's not that bad.

THE BEST!

BEST MOVE *Honorable Mention*:
Allowing SP Pedro Martinez to leave for the New York Mets after the 2004 season.

At the time, Red Sox Nation wasn't ready to let go of Pedro. The Sox had just won their first World Series title in 86 years, and although Pedro was no longer dominant, he continued to get the job done. However, behind the scenes, Pedro clashed with Theo and the rest of his front office mates (he once called them a bunch of "stat geeks"), and his physical deterioration had become overtly clear to Boston's baseball people. Pedro's fastball had dipped consistently into the low 90s, and his big, sweeping curveball had lost some of its effectiveness.

Still, Pedro was a solid major league starting pitcher. Theo did the right thing; he extended an offer, but not a ridiculous one: three years, $30.5 million. The problem was that word had traveled around the league that the Mets were already offering Pedro a four-year contract worth significantly more than $10 million per season. Theo knew he was low-balling Pedro, but took a shot anyway.

His shot bricked and careened wildly off the backboard. Pedro was insulted by the offer, and had his metaphorical middle finger in the air as he left town. His first year with the Mets was an excellent one; Pedro went 15-8 with 208 strikeouts and four complete games on a team that failed to reach the postseason.

Since then Pedro's been nothing but a headache for Mets' management and fans. His body is a mess. The veteran right-hander from the Dominican Republic has had hip problems, repeated shoulder stiffness, a calf tear, a strained hamstring, torn rotator cuff, and he's even spent time on the bereavement list. The Mets have never had the opportunity to run Pedro out there for an extended period of time, and even when he makes it to the hill, his stuff just isn't what it used to be. Not even close, really.

To be specific, Pedro went from 217 innings pitched in '05, to 132 in '06, down to 28 in '07. Making over $13 million a season with the Mets, it's almost like he's stealing money. In 2008, Pedro threw only 109 innings for the Metropolitans.

Theo was right to be cautious with his offer to Pedro; the only reason this decision didn't crack the top five is because Theo replaced him with Matt Clement. Let one questionable guy go, bring in another—can't get too much credit for that.

BEST MOVE # 5
Signing RP Hideki Okajima to a two-year deal worth less than $3 million.

Talk about a steal. The left-hander was one of the top relievers in Japan for a long time, and was still only 31 years old when Theo got him to sign on the dotted line. With his unorthodox delivery, outstanding off-speed stuff—an overhand curve, splitter, and change-up—and well-located fastball, Okajima has been one of the best relievers in the bigs over the course of the past two seasons.

Okajima was selected to the American League All-Star team in his rookie season, and finished the year with a pretty 2.22 ERA. His strikeout rate was surprisingly solid considering the mediocrity of his fastball: 63 Ks in 69 innings. It seemed as if major league hitters had figured Okajima out at the beginning of this season, but the crafty lefty has since made some fine adjustments. In 2008, his ERA was very credible at 2.61.

Okajima is incredibly consistent—he was 3-2 in '07, and 3-2 in '08; he was six strikeouts below his innings pitched last year, and two below in '08; he gave up six homers last season and six again in '08. Theo and Terry Francona know what to expect from their eighth inning man, and they get it: exceptional work and the versatility to get both lefties and righties out. In the era of bullpen specialization, Okajima is a rare gem. Theo found a diamond in the rough.

BEST MOVE # 4
Firing Manager Grady Little and replacing him with Terry Francona.

This is the most controversial selection on either end of the list. Why? Because it's impossible to know if the Red

Sox would have won the World Series with Little as their manager in 2004. They were outs away from the big dance in '03, and Theo improved his roster talent in the ensuing off-season. Had Little inherited the '04 team, he could have duplicated Francona's success. Either way, it's purely speculation.

Since taking over the helm, Francona has done an incredible job of managing the multitude of personalities on his ball club; however, he took plenty of heat for his decision-making during the '04 regular season. Maybe it was because he was the new blood, or maybe it was a fan and media hangover from Little's decision to stick with Pedro in the ALCS, but whatever it was, Terry had to earn his stripes.

In the playoffs, he did. The statisticians at Baseball Prospectus, some of the most trusted and thorough in the world, said the 2004 ALCS featured one of the most lopsided managerial battles in the history of baseball. They gave Francona the razor-sharp edge over the Yankees' skipper, four-time World Series champion Joe Torre. In short, Francona completely outmanaged Torre, both practically and statistically. In his own way, Francona was just as responsible for the Red Sox's historic comeback as Dave Roberts, Pedro Martinez, Keith Foulke, Curt Schilling, and even David Ortiz. Ultimately the players have to execute, but it's the manager who places them in the position to do so.

Manager Terry Francona and Theo

Four years later, Francona has more "stripes" than the 1981 Bill Murray film. In Boston, it's in Tito they trust. If Theo and GM Kevin Towers were "TNT" in San Diego, then Theo and Tito are the second coming in Beantown. "TNT2," however, is much more explosive; the tandem has an excellent relationship off the field, as well.

As for Grady Little, he went on to manage the Los Angeles Dodgers in '06 and '07. In his first year on the job, he led his team to an 88-74 record and a victory in the wacky Wild Card race. However, Little fell short again in the postseason when the Mets swept his boys in the National League Division Series.

The connections to Theo and the Red Sox—past and

future—were everywhere: Nomar Garciaparra was the Dodgers' shortstop, J.D. Drew was in right field, Derek Lowe was one of the starting pitchers, and Bill Mueller and Julio Lugo were both on the roster. When Little was fired after a disappointing 2007 season, he was replaced by none other than… Joe Torre. How fitting.

BEST MOVE # 3

Trading SS Nomar Garciaparra and netting SS Orlando Cabrera and 1B Doug Mientkiewicz.

"Trading Nomar? That takes guts," Padres' GM Kevin Towers said. "That takes huge guts, but Theo did what he thought was right for the organization and it worked."

Towers was absolutely right, it takes a confident and courageous executive to trade the face of a franchise. That's exactly what Theo did when he dealt Nomar to the Chicago Cubs in the midst of the 2004 regular season, but that's not all he did…

In the process, Theo broke the hearts of thousands upon thousands of Red Sox fans who absolutely adored their shortstop, "Number Five." Nomar crushed over 20 homeruns six times with the Red Sox, and hit .300 or better in seven different seasons, including the year in which he was traded. In his prime, Nomar was one-third of a triumvirate of incredible American League shortstops, the others being Alex Rodriguez and Derek Jeter. The trio set new standards for offensive shortstops, and represented the changing nature of the game.

When Theo sent Nomar packing, he was batting .321 and seemed comfortable as ever in the batters' box. Ted Williams, the greatest Red Sock of all time, a sweet-swinging left-handed hitter who hit .406 in 1941, once said that Nomar was the only player in the world who could follow in his footsteps. In a way, Teddy Ballgame had made Nomar "The Chosen One" in Boston, so how did it get to the point where Theo "knew" he had to trade him?

There were three factors: Nomar's defense, health, and attitude. The multiple injuries he suffered through cut his range in half, there was a legitimate risk of re-aggravation or an entirely new injury, and he was still steaming about Theo's off-season attempt to replace him with A-Rod. Nomar had become a pouter and complainer, and refused to be understanding about the fact that Theo was pursuing the best player in the world, not some mediocre shortstop who couldn't shine Nomar's shoes.

After a meeting involving Larry Lucchino, Theo, and Nomar, it became clear to the execs that it was time to move on to the next Red Sox shortstop. Instead of working things out and telling his bosses that everything would be OK, Nomar continued to harp on A-Rod and the subsequent trade that would have sent him to the White Sox for right fielder Magglio Ordonez.

With the meeting, injuries, and shaky defense in

mind, Theo sent away a Red Sox legend. He brought back two fine defensive players, shortstop Orlando Cabrera and first baseman Doug Mientkiewicz. Cabrera went on to do a phenomenal job—both offensively and defensively—as the everyday replacement for Nomar, and Mientkiewicz became a valuable late-inning defensive substitution for Kevin Millar. Nomar proceeded to drop down to .297 with the Cubbies, and played in only 81 total games for the season.

In the end, this may be remembered as the defining trade of Theo's career. He knew he would take an immense amount of heat for dealing such a high-profile player, but it was heat he was willing to take in order to improve the defense and chemistry of his team. Theo never once fed Nomar to the wolves by telling the media that he had become a cancer in the clubhouse.

If Nomar had stayed healthy, played well for the Cubs and the Red Sox missed the playoffs, it would have been Theo's head. But he rolled the dice, and came up seven.

As is always the case with Theo, it was a calculated risk.

BEST MOVE #2

Trading SS Hanley Ramirex and SP Anibal Sanchez to the Florida Marlins for SP John Beckett and 3B Mike Lowell.

This trade comes with an asterisk, because it was completed during Theo's time away from the Red Sox. However, Bill Lajoie, who was assistant to the general manager at the time, said he "knew what Theo wanted" from the deal.

Theo's philosophy has always been to build from within, with a strong minor league system. Evaluating prospects and projecting their production in the bigs can be a slippery slope; with this trade, Boston opted for the proven major league talent. It wasn't an easy decision; some scouts were comparing Ramirez's offensive ability to A-Rod's. A player similar to the shortstop Theo had always wanted was waiting down in Double-A, but there were questions about his defense and plate discipline.

The Red Sox didn't have the time to wait for Ramirez to develop the cerebral part of his game. Their starting rotation was shaky, and with a 25-year-old stud like Beckett available, there was no room for hesitation. The Yankees had been snatching up players who had impressed them in the playoffs—think Jason Giambi with the Athletics, Randy Johnson with the Diamondbacks, Carl Pavano with the Marlins, and Johnny Damon with the Red Sox— and Beckett absolutely dominated the Bombers in the '02 World Series. There was reason to believe that Brian Cashman would make a push for him.

So the Sox packaged their best offensive prospect with Sanchez, one of their top minor league arms, and made an offer the Marlins couldn't refuse. Florida was looking to cut payroll and build a team of talented young players, and Ramirez and Sanchez were perfect fits. In addition, they wanted Boston to eat much of Lowell's hefty contract, and Boston didn't mind. Lowell was coming off a down year, but was still a slick glove and natural hitter who could befriend the Green Monster. He was an expensive throw-in, but a potentially useful one.

Boston's front office recognized that in the era of the longball and American League lineups that hit one through nine, bona fide aces were nearly impossible to come by. Beckett hadn't yet proven himself as a regular-season No. 1, but had done so in the playoffs. His devastating arsenal of pitches and bulldog mentality suggested that it wouldn't be long before his dominance spanned the course of a full season.

That season would be 2007, a year in which he went 20-7 with a 3.27 ERA and 194 strikeouts, en route to a spot on the All-Star team and the ALCS MVP Award. If that wasn't enough to make this move one of the best of Theo's tenure, Lowell sealed the deal by hitting .324 with 21 homers and 120 RBI and bringing home the World Series MVP trophy. Beckett and Lowell were arguably the most important and valuable players on the 2007 world champion Red Sox.

In one hell of a trade, the Red Sox snagged them both.

BEST MOVE #1

Signing 1B/DH David Ortiz to a one-year contract worth 1.25 million.

Any time you can sign a guy for $1.25 million, blink, and he becomes one of the premier hitters in baseball, you should be dancing naked in the streets.

All right, maybe that's a little too extreme, but the Ortiz signing was worth a victory parade, or at least an end-zone celebration. For starters, he was coming off his best season in '03, a year in which he hit 20 homers and 75 RBI while slugging .500—all career highs. From the start, $1.25 million looked like a bargain for Ortiz.

The signing went from a bargain to the greatest thing since sliced bread when Papi hit .288 with 31 homers and 101 RBI in 2004. He proceeded to become the superhero of the postseason, and deserves the most recognition for Boston's earth-shattering 0-3 comeback against the Yankees.

Credit Theo for understanding that Ortiz could reach his full potential with the help of Fenway's short porch in right and the big, ugly, green wall in left. Papi had shown the ability to take the ball the other way, and that's a can't-miss quality for a left-handed hitter who plays his home games in Boston.

From left to right:
Manager Terry Francona, hitting coach Dave Magadan, David Ortiz,

GM Theo Epstein, Dustin Pedroia, and Kevin Youkilis

THEO-LOGY

It was once Nomar; at times Pedro Martinez and Manny Ramirez; but with all three gone, David Ortiz is now the face of the Boston Red Sox.

Or perhaps… Theo is.

So do the great moves outweigh the horrific? It's certainly difficult to argue with Theo's results—two World Series titles and five postseason berths in six years—but who is to say that another GM wouldn't have won three or four championships if given the same talent and financial resources? Like the Grady Little/Terry Francona situation, there is no way of knowing. But to be fair to Theo, there is something else to consider:

The strength of his minor league system. It can't be considered a single move or transaction, but Theo's insistence that players be cultivated, groomed, and promoted through the ranks of the Red Sox's farm has turned Boston's roster into one with great balance and staying power.

On Theo's 2008 club, there was second baseman Dustin Pedroia, a second round draft pick in 2004; centerfielder Jacoby Ellsbury, a first round selection in '05; shortstop Jed Lowrie, a supplemental first rounder in '05; starting pitcher Clay Buchholz, another '05 first rounder; starter Michael Bowden, a second supplemental first rounder in '05, and starter/reliever Justin Masterson, a second rounder in '06.

The first of that bunch, Pedroia, was named 2008 American League Most Valuable Player. In just his second-full season, the sensationally scrappy second baseman hit

.326 with 17 homers, 83 RBI, 213 hits, 54 doubles, and 20 stolen bases. Pedroia was second to Joe Mauer (.328) in batting average, and also won the Gold Glove at his position. This all coming after winning the AL Rookie of the Year Award in 2007. Talk about a find for Theo.

All things considered, Theo has managed to build a bright future for the Red Sox, without compromising the present. Boston is a World Series contender this season, and another championship could be on the horizon.

Is Theo Epstein a spectacular general manager? Or are the bottomless wallets of John Henry and Tom Werner responsible for the revival of the Boston Red Sox?

That's for you to decide.

The World in His Palm

F ew 34-year-olds have accomplished what Theo Epstein has. He boasts an undergraduate degree from Yale—an Ivy League school—and a law degree from the University of San Diego. He passed the California bar exam on his first try, and worked his way up from Baltimore Orioles intern to San Diego Padres director of Baseball Operations to Boston Red Sox general manager. Since taking over as the youngest GM in Major League Baseball history, he's reached the playoffs five times in six years, and won two World Series titles.

Theo was an essential contributor to the rainstorm that ended Boston's 86-year World Series drought, and is no longer considered a "boy" or "kid." He is now regarded as one of the more brilliant and efficient *men* in all of baseball.

But is baseball enough?

As Bill Lajoie said of Theo, "The man has the ability to lead this country."

Is he being wasted in baseball?

Those who love the game as much as Theo does would never put "waste" in the same sentence as "baseball." During his days at Yale, Theo told friends and coworkers that he would eventually become the Boston Red Sox's general manager; that was his dream job. In the sixth official year of his dream, it's difficult to imagine Theo leaving the job. He walked away once, and sprinted back quickly. That first love is always difficult to shake.

Theo inked a new deal with the Red Sox prior to 2009's annual GM meetings. As usual, he mentioned it casually, and didn't give away any details.

"We finished it weeks ago," he told reporters in early November. "I can't remember when."

With his new contract and track record of success, Theo may very well be a baseball "lifer," one who never leaves the game. But who knows? With his mind, the way he presents himself and handles others, anything is possible.

* * *

"Of course, there are those who learn after the first few times. They grow out of sports. And there are others who were born with the wisdom to know that nothing lasts. These are the truly tough among us, the ones who can live without illusion, or without even the hope of illusion. I am not that grown-up or up-to-date. I am a simpler creature, tied to more primitive patterns and cycles. I need to think something lasts forever, and it might as well be that state of being that is a game; it might as well be that, in a green field, in the sun."

-A. Bartlett Giamatti

Bibliography

"AFI's 100 Years…100 Movies." The American Film Institute. http://www. afi.com/tvevents/100years/movies.aspx.

"Anya Epstein." IMDB: The Internet Movie Database. http://www.imdb. com/name/nm0258425/.

Associated Press, "Bosox sent Arroyo and cash to Reds for Pena." ESPN.com, March 20, 2006. http://sports.espn.go.com/mlb/news/story?id=2376683.

Associated Press, "Drew agrees with Boston on $70 million, 5-year deal." ESPN.com, December 7, 2006. http://sports.espn.go.com/mlb/news/ story?id=2687740.

Associated Press. "Epstein leaves Red Sox without a GM." ESPN.com, November 1, 2005. http://sports.espn.go.com/mlb/news/story?id=2209574.

Associated Press. "Epstein's promotion completes front office overhaul." ESPN.com, November 25, 2002. http://espn.go.com/.

Associated Press. "Meet Boston GM Theo Epstein." *USA Today*, November 30, 2002. http://asp.usatoday.com/sports/baseball/al/redsox/2002-11-30-epstein-feature_x.htm.

Associated Press. "Theo Epstein and wife welcome a boy, Jack." BostonHerald.com, December 12, 2007. http://www.bostonherald.com/ sports/baseball/red_sox/view.bg?articleid=1050413.

Baram, Marcus. "Theo in Love." *Boston Magazine*, November 2006. http:// www.bostonmagazine.com/arts_entertainment/articles/theo_in_love/.

"Bart Giamatti." NNDB.com. http://www.nndb.com/people/807/000044675/.

"Beane had Red Sox Deal, but decides to stay with A's." ESPN.com, November 11, 2002. http://espn.go.com/.

Bellafante, Ginia. "A New-Age General Manager Helps End an Age-Old Curse." *New York Times,* October 28 2004. http://www.nytimes.com/2004/10/28/ sports/baseball/28theo.html?_r=2&oref=slogin&oref=slogin.

Burt, Bill. "Mistreated at 33 years old..." *Eagle-Tribune,* October 23, 2007. http://www.eagletribune.com/pusports/local_story_296121207.

"Biography for Theo Epstein." IMDB: The Internet Movie Database. http://www.imdb.com/name/nm1795393/bio.

Bock, Hal. "Papelbon to Boston's rescue." MLB.com, June 12, 2006. http://boston.redsox.mlb.com/news/article.jsp?ymd=20060612&content_id=1501569&vkey=news_bos&fext=.jsp&c_id=bos.

"Boston's blow out caps unequaled comeback." ESPN.com. http://sports.espn.go.com/mlb/recap?gameId=241020110.

Browne, Ian. "Francona named Red Sox manager." MLB.com, December 4, 2003. http://mlb.mlb.com/news/article.jsp?ymd=20031204&content_id=611819&vkey=news_mlb&fext=.jsp&c_id=mlb.

Browne, Ian. "Garciaparra traded to Cubs." MLB.com, July 31, 2004. http://redsox.mlb.com/news/article.jsp?ymd=20040731&content_id=815282&vkey=news_bos&fext=.jsp&c_id=bos.

Browne, Ian. "Red Sox Sign Ortiz to One-Year Deal." MLB.com, January 21, 2003. http://redsox.mlb.com/news/.

Browne, Ian. "Sox unveil Matsuzaka." MLB.com, December 14, 2006. http://boston.redsox.mlb.com/news/article.isp?ymd=20061214&content_id=1761085&vkey=news_bos&fext=.jsp&c_id=bos.

Chass, Murray. "New G.M. Of Red Sox is Youngest In History." *New York Times,* November 26, 2002. http://query.nytimes.com/gst/fullpage.html?res=9D07E6D91F39F935A15752C1A9649C8B63&sec=&spon=&pagewanted=1.

Cohen, Sonja. "Red Sox Sign National Treasure Daisuke Matsuzaka." About.com. http://boston.about.com/od/professionalsports/a/matsuzakasigned.htm.

Curry, Jack. "Brian Cashman and Theo Epstein Talk Baseball." *New York Times,* January 26, 2008. http://bats.blogs.nytimes.com/2008/01/26/brian-cashman-and-theo-epstein-talk-baseball/.

Curry, Jack. "Theo Epstein's Mistake." *New York Times,* March 14, 2008. http://bats.blogs.nytimes.com/2008/03/14/theo-epsteins-mistake/.

"Dan Futterman." IMDB: The Internet Movie Database. http://www.imdb.com/name/nm0001246/.

DiMeglio, Steve. "Papelbon's stuff impresses Red Sox." *USA Today,* April 11, 2006. http://www.usatoday.com/sports/baseball/al/redsox/2006-04-11-papelbon_x.htm.

Edes, Gordon. "Beckett signs deal to remain through 2009." *Boston Globe,* July 20, 2006. http://www.boston.com/sports/baseball/redsox/articles/2006/07/20/beckett_signs_deal_to_remain_through_2009/.

Edes, Gordon and Snow, Chris. "Epstein rejects upgraded offer from Sox." *Boston Globe,* October 26, 2005. http://www.boston.com/sports/baseball/redsox/articles/2005/10/26/epstein_rejects_upgraded_offer_from_sox/.

Edes, Gordon. "Hitch was in his plan." *Boston Globe,* January 31, 2001. http://www.boston.com/sports/baseball/redsox/articles/2007/01/31/hitch_was_in_his_plan/.

Edes, Gordon. "Inner workings revealed." *Boston Globe,* July 7, 2006. http://www.boston.com/sports/baseball/redsox/articles/2006/07/07/inner_workings_revealed/.

Edes, Gordon. "Void is filled with Clement." *Boston Globe,* December 18, 2004. http://www.boston.com/sports/baseball/redsox/articles/2004/12/18/void_is_filled_with_clement/.

"Epstein Marriage At Hot Dog Stand A 'Joke,' Paper Says." WCVBTV, January 31, 2007. http://www.thebostonchannel.com/sports/10888395/detail.html?rss=bos&psp=news.

Giamatti, A. Bartlett. "The Green Fields of the Mind," in *A Great and Glorious Game: Baseball Writings of A. Bartlett Giamatti.* Edited by Kenneth S. Robson. Chapel Hill: Algonquin Books, 1998.

Goldman, Steven and Baseball Prospectus Team of Experts. *Mind Game: How the Boston Red Sox Got Smart, Won a World Series, and Created a New Blueprint for Winning.* New York: Workman Publishing Company Inc., 2005.

Gopisetty, Smita. "For Epstein '95, a dream fulfilled at 28." *Yale Daily News,* December 11, 2002. http://www.yaledailynews.com/articles/view/6286?badlink=1.

Gray, Scott. *The Mind of Bill James: How a Complete Outsider Changed Baseball.* New York: Doubleday, 2006.

"Hoyer, Cherington named co-GMs." ESPN.com, December 13, 2005. http://sports.espn.go.com/mlb/news/story?id=2256622.

Horrigan, Jeff. "The Story." Peter Gammons' Hot Stove, Cool Music, September 2003. http://hotstovecoolmusic.org/story/index.html.

James, Bill. *The New Bill James Historical Baseball Abstract.* New York: Free Press, 2003.

Lat, David. "The Bar Exam: A List of Famous Failures." *Above the Law: A Legal Tabloid,* July 7, 2007. http://www.abovethelaw.com/2007/07/the_bar_exam_a_list_of famous_1.php.

"Matsuzaka, Red Sox reach agreement on six-year deal." ESPN.com, February 23, 2007. http://sports.espn.go.com/mlb/news/story?id=2696321.

Mitchell, George J. *Report to the Commissioner of Baseball of an Independent Investigation Into the Illegal Use of Steroids and Other Performance Enhancing Substances by Players in Major League Baseball.* December 13, 2007. http://assets.espn.go.com/media/pdf/071213/mitchell_report.pdf.

Mullen, Maureen. "Rockin' Gammons returns to the stage." MLB.com, January 8, 2007. http://boston.redsox.mlb.com/news/article.jsp?ymd=2007 0108&contentid=1774708&vkey=news_bos&fext=.jsp&c_id=bos.

"Obama for America." *NNDB: tracking the entire world.* http://www.nndb.com/org/684/000167183/.

Passan, Jeff. "A monkey off Theo's back." Yahoo Sports.com, May 22, 2006. http://sports.yahoo.com/mlb/news?slug=jp-epstein052206&prov=yhoo&type=lgns.

Passan, Jeff. "Two Series titles evidence of growing Theo-logy." Yahoo Sports.com, November 26, 2007. http://sports.yahoo.com/mlb/news?slug=jp-theo112707&prov=yhoo&type=lgns.

"Paul Giamatti." IMDB: The Internet Movie Database. http://www.imdb.com/name/nm0316079/.

Petraglia, Mike. "Sox sign Japanese lefty Okajima." MLB.com, November 30, 2006. http://mlb.mlb.com/news/article.jsp?ymd=20061130&content_id=1748009&vkey=news_bos&fext=.jsp&c_id=bos.

"Philip G. Epstein." IMDB: The Internet Movie Database. http://www.imdb.com/name/nm0258525/.

"Press Release: Theo Epstein rejoins Red Sox as Executive Vice President/ General Manager." MLB.com, January 24, 2006. http://boston.redsox. mlb.com/news/press_releases/press_release.jsp?ymd=20060124&content_ id=1300064&vkey=pr_bos&fext=.jsp&c_id=bos.

"Red Sox complete deal for Beckett, Lowell." ESPN.com, November 25, 2005. http://sports.espn.go.com/mlb/news/story?id=2232211.

"Red Sox, GM Epstein agree to new contract." *USA Today,* November 4, 2008. http://www.boston.com/sports/baseball/redsox/articles/2006/07/20/ beckett_signs_deal_to_remain_through_2009/.

"Red Sox GM Epstein gets married on owner's yacht." ESPN.com, January 31, 2007. http://theo-epstein-news.newslib.com/story/5978-3199600/.

"Red Sox GM Theo Epstein Gets Married." *Give Me My Remote,* January 31, 2007. http://www.givememyremote.com/remote/red-sox-gm-theo-epstein-gets-married/.

"Red Sox upgrade bullpen with Gagné deal." MLB.com, July 30, 2007. http://sports.espn.go.com/mlb/news/story?id=2955966.

Ryan, Bob. "City's Pain Will Last, but Manager Won't." *Boston Globe* via *New York Times* online, October 18, 2003. http://query.nytimes.com/gst/ fullpage.html?res=9B06E7D9123EF93BA25753C1A9659C8B63&n=Top/ Reference/Times%20Topics/People/L/Little,%20Grady.

Shanahan, Mark. "Epstein's wife gives birth to baby boy." *Boston Globe,* December 12, 2007. http://www.boston.com/sports/baseball/redsox/ articles/2007/12/12/epsteins_wife_gives_birth_to_baby_boy/.

Shaughnessy, Dan. "Let's iron out some of this dirty laundry." *Boston Globe,* October 30, 2005. http://www.boston.com/sports/baseball/redsox/ articles/2005/10/30/lets_iron_out_some_of_this_dirty_laundry/.

Shaughnessy, Dan. *Reversing the Curse.* New York: Houghton Mifflin Harcourt, 2005.

Simmons, Bill. "Prodigal son, departs." ESPN.com. http://proxy.espn. go.com/espn/page2/story?page=simmons/051101.

Snow, Chris. "Source: Sox agree to Crisp deal." *Boston Globe,* January 23, 2006. http://www.boston.com/sports/baseball/redsox/articles/2006/01/23/source_sox_agree_to_crisp_deal/.

Sports Reference LLC. Baseball-Reference.com, 2000-2009. http://www.baseball-reference.com.

Sports Reference LLC. "Calvin Hill." Pro-Football-Reference.com, 2000-2009, http://www.pro-football-reference.com/ players/H/HillCa00.htm

"Statement from Lucchino regarding Players Association decision." MLB.com, December 17, 2003. http://redsox.mlb.com/news/article.jsp?ymd=20031217&content_id=620341&vkey=news_bos&fext=.jsp&c_id=bos.

"A statement from Theo Epstein." MLB.com, October 31, 2005. http://boston.redsox.mlb.com/news/article.jsp?ymd=20051031&content_id=1262977&vkey=news_bos&fext=.jsp&c_id=bos.

Swidey, Neil. "The Architect." *Boston Globe,* December 26, 2004. http://www.boston.com/news/globe/magazine/articles/2004/12/26/the_architect/.

Thamel, Pete. "BASEBALL: The Red Sox Part Ways With Little." *New York Times,* October 28, 2003. http://query.nytimes.com/gst/fullpage.html?res=9C01EED71E31F93BA15753C1A9659C8B63.

"Theo Epstein talks about his team's postseason hot streak." (MP3 audio file), ESPN.com. http://sports.espn.go.com/espnradio/player?context=audio&id=3084744.

"Theo's Gorilla Suit Fetches $11,000 At Auction." WBZTV, January 9, 2009. http://wbztv.com/sports/Theo.Epstein.Gorilla.2.575502.html.

Subject Index

INDEX

INDEX

INDEX